YOU CAN

Unleash Your Inner

Diva

Stephanie Beattie

Copyright © 2009 by Representing All Women

All rights reserved. No part of this book may be reproduced in any form or by any electronic or mechanical means, including information storage and retrieval systems, without permission in writing from the publisher, except by a reviewer who may quote brief passages in a review.

Published by:

Representing ALL WOMEN

259 A Innisfil Street
Barrie, Ontario L4N 3G2
www.representingallwomen.com

Book cover and text design by:
Expressions Custom Publications
www.expressionscustompublications.com

ISBN: 978-0-9812040-0-0

All rights reserved.
Printed in Canada.
First Edition.

Dedication

This book is dedicated to
all the women who have touched my life,
who have allowed me to grow and learn,
and who made me who I am.

TABLE OF CONTENTS

Dedication	5
Foreword	11
My Story	13
What Is An Inner Diva?	17
Begin Your Diva Quest	19
Your Inner Diva Quest Quiz	21
Discovering Your Inner Diva	23
Diva Passion Meter Quiz	27
Diva Power & Passion	29
Diva Passion Meter Quiz	33
Diva Types	37
The Creative Diva	38
The Domestic Diva	40
Social Diva	42
The Business Diva	45
The Balanced Diva	47
Curiouser and Curiouser	49
Draw A Circle	51
Forgive To Live!	53
Shaboo On!	57
Hire The Coach	61
Take Care of You!	63
Lost In The Clouds	69
Dream On!	73
It's Great To Be You!	77
Make Your Dreams Come True	79
Mistakes Were Made	83

TABLE OF CONTENTS

Little Voices 85
Power Up! 89
Celebrate Being A Woman 93
Detox Your Relationships 95
Self Respect – Even My body 99
An Abundant Life 101
So Much To Give 103
Live Rich 105
Give It Away 107
Enjoy Your Successes 109
Today Is My Choice 111
Live Your Values 113
Dress Like You Mean It 115
Diva At Work 119
Speak Like A Diva! 123
Starting A New Job 127
The Interview Wardrobe 129
The Past and Future 131
Men And Their Divas 133
So What If It's A Man's World! 135
So You're In High School! 137
On My Own 139
Some Rules for Success 141
Finally 143
Famous Women 145
Helpful Resources 147
How Can I Help You? 149

Foreword

The goal of this book is to help you understand what it means to discover and unleash your inner diva. That is a journey that is different for each of us. I'll share with you some of the experiences I have had on my journey from a very simple beginning to my present life as a successful business woman, inspiring speaker, coach and mother.

Once we have made that discovery, we will realize that we are one of the major types of diva that make up our world. Each one has its strengths and weaknesses. That means we need each other!

I'll also include some of the advice I have received along the way and some things that I have faced that might be helpful for your journey.

There are many helpful resources available to all of us and I've included many of those for you to explore.

So, let's begin our quest to discover and unleash your inner diva!

My Story

I have always believed in one rule "It's right if it works". The first company I launched was started with $40.00 in my pocket. I grew it to over a million dollars. I did it on my own, and it was successful because of one major, important, key, specific ingredient... ME. But success does not come without challenges.

I remember many, many years ago when I applied to the bank for a credit card. I didn't actually know what it was for but like most young people my age I felt that I needed one. At the time, I was a waitress and earning less than the usual minimum wage. As you know if you have ever been a waitress, you receive a small hourly rate of pay and then it is expected that you will make the difference between that and good money through tips. It's an incentive for the waitress – and a huge risk if you are not a people person who can make people feel good as well as get their correct order to them quickly. In my case, I was doing well for myself and was receiving excellent tips from my customers.

After going through the application process, like most people I was excited about the possibility of having my own credit card. Wouldn't it be great to be the one putting a credit card down at the restaurant? Goodness knows that I've picked up enough credit cards over the years as a waitress. It was another step in becoming an adult.

The bank declined me.

I was devastated and confused. Why would they decline me? I worked hard. I paid my bills. I had money in the bank. I had to find out. I felt embarrassed as I made the appointment to talk to someone at the bank.

I sat down feeling like a student at the principal's office when you were in trouble but you know that you didn't do anything wrong. Then with the paperwork in front of her, the banking officer looked up and gave me the reason for the bank's decision.

I was declined because I had an "unskilled" job.

My head started swimming. Here was this woman telling me that I had an unskilled job and was not credit worthy. I just about had an out of body experience. What could I say? What should I say? What would I say? I wasn't sure and then it happened.

I leaned over the desk. In my kindest, gentlest, most thoughtful voice I said "I make more money than you do".

In 48 hours I had my credit card.

Over the years, I had wondered what I would have to do to have a skilled job to become this mega-mogul that I had always dreamed of becoming. I knew I wanted a certain lifestyle. I wanted to be rich with a family. I wanted to have lots of friends. Did I mention money...lol? I wanted to be that story that people talked about who actually made it.

This book is now part of that story. It is my way of acknowledging at a point in time that I made it and made it big. I became all that I wanted to be. I have all that I dreamed about. And I did it on my own.

Growing up, I know my family life was far from being glamorous and fulfilled. My family life was sometimes hard. It was full of difficult experiences and disappointments. It was not easy being me as a kid. We grew up thinking that it was somehow bad to have big dreams. It was like the worst thing that could happen to you was becoming rich and famous. Even as I write this, my family believes that money and wealth is a negative bad thing. "It breeds greed and everyone I know who has ever had it never did anything good with it," my mom used to say.

When did it become such a bad thing?

If a woman is seen as a go-getter and wanting too much – it is perceived as a negative thing. If you aim too high, people will look down on you for that. I'm sure there are probably psychological and historical reasons for that. People get stuck in fear of failure and fear of disappointment. Their potential as people is trapped. It is as if their inner self – their inner diva is in chains.

Without aspirations, bigger and better dreams for a more enriched life, you are never going to achieve much. You're always going to be going nowhere.

Why not dream big? Stop sleep walking through your life and wake up. You are already a diva. She is buried deep inside you waiting to be unleashed.

I have always visualized that this day would come for me. I knew that through all that I felt, wanted, pursued, and envisioned my dream would come true. I knew something great would happen in my life. My many career paths have included changes and the road has not always been easy but I'm now at the point where people ask me how they can get where I am.

So here we are.

No matter where you are in your journey – just beginning, trapped in a rut, well on your way up the mountain or standing on a peak looking at the next mountain – this book will help you too. Consider this your passport, passport to something fresh and new, fun or glamorous, that you can take with you. The ultimate is self empowerment, self reliance and self love. This book was written for you. Let's move forward on our journey together. Choose to begin now - ready or not! It's time for you to have it all. Unleash your inner diva!

What Is An Inner Diva?

You may be one of the many people who wonder – what is my "inner diva" anyway?

You may have heard the term "diva" used as a negative referring to someone who is self-absorbed, difficult, manipulative and fussy who want to grab the spotlight. It is opera's version of a "prima donna" with all the arrogant associations involved with that term.

More and more you may have heard it in a positive way which gets us back to its original meaning. The positive context of the word is associated with the Italian use of the word that referred to a rare and spectacular talent first used with opera but also applied to popular music, theater and other performing arts.

If we want to go back even further we can find the original root word in Latin which was the feminine form of the word "divus" which meant godlike or divine. So for the word diva – we are talking about the idea of a "goddess."

For our purposes in this book – we are after the positive idea of something "inspired" or "divinely given" to each of us as women. These "gifts" that we have all been given as women give us some special abilities or potential to sense, share and shape the world around us. These gifts are where we find the passions in our life. Those passions once discovered, nurtured and channeled into our world bring a special beauty and grace to everything we are and everything we do.

We can talk about our inner diva as a "she" deep inside us. She is that little voice we used to hear so clearly as a child but need to learn to hear again as we become women. Our inner diva is that voice that whispers to us that we are special – and that we can do something special. It is the voice that keeps calling to us to reach our potential as women and to make a difference in our world.

Women who have found their inner diva understand that in addition to the many things they can be and do in life – they have a special calling and need to concentrate in an area of life. These women are no longer satisfied to just trudge through the daily routines. They understand that there is so much more to experience about themselves and the life around them. They have made the connection!

Our inner diva is very much connected to the best of our childhood. Think of what it means to be a child. It is a time of wonder. It is a time where everything is new. The world awaits us! We can explore the endless possibilities of our environment. We are not burdened by our history or experiences. We can be anything we choose to be. Our imagination is unhindered by the adult realities that will soon intrude on us. We wake up each day where our only mission in life is to be a kid.

Each inner diva is as unique as we are. It is shaped by the experiences, times and places of our lives. But it is like a seed lying dormant under the snow – waiting for the springtime to give it the warmth and rain to sprout and grow. With nurturing and support – this inner diva can produce a special fruit that will enrich the world around us.

If you are one of those people who are frustrated with where you are in life right now, if you are not content with spending the rest of your life feeling like you do right now – read on. There is hope! The winter season of your life where everything seems to feel dead and dreary is ready to give way to an enchanted spring!

Get ready for the awakening!

Begin Your Diva Quest

It begins with a stirring sensation. Something is awakening from a long sleep. The hibernation is ending and it is time to leave that cave and re-enter the world out there.

There is a part of us that just wants to stay where we are. It may not be great but I know what it is. It is familiar. It's even cozy at times. I feel safe in my routines. If I venture out – who knows what might happen?

But your inner diva will not give up. You feel that nudge. There is an urge to reach out for more than what you are today. Like a great stretch – your body is telling you it is time to get moving.

The diva quest has begun.

For some women – that's where it will end. They never move beyond those stirring feelings that are calling you to move outside of where you are. The fear of the unknown or the weight and discouragement of life make them feel like it is not worth the struggle. They are bound by the chains of a life lived in the grey fog of what others have told them is normal or expected of them. The world is littered with these sad souls who have withered over years of saying no to the call of their inner diva. Finally, that inner voice becomes harder and harder to hear. Then we wonder what that faint noise is. Finally, we get to a place where we are not sure we ever really heard anything.

But it does not have to be this way for you! If we are not growing we are dying. If you want more out of life and are no longer willing to accept the status quo – then the diva quest awaits you!

No matter who you are, where you live, whether you are rich or poor, whether you are old or young – you can discover your inner diva. You can experience the gift that you have been given that gives you a new sense of fulfillment and possibilities! Like any great quest – it begins with a simple decision – I'll go!

You may not have all the answers – in fact no one does. You may not know where you'll end up. That's OK too. This is a journey that will take a lifetime but will bring you a new sense of meaning and purpose in your days. So have courage. Decide to go on this quest!

Your Inner Diva Quest Quiz

Take this first quiz to explore how well you know your inner diva! Count how many of the following statements are true for you right now. The score key to interpret your results will follow. Total your score from 0-10.

- [ ] I enjoy being a woman.
- [ ] I know myself as a woman.
- [ ] I have a clear sense of who I am as a woman.
- [ ] I understand my special strengths as a woman.
- [ ] I know what makes me satisfied in life.
- [ ] I am a basically happy person.
- [ ] I have discovered my calling as a person.
- [ ] If my life ended today, I could say I had a good life.
- [ ] I know that I make a difference in my world.
- [ ] I am a positive person.

What Was Your Inner Diva Quest Score?

Take your total score from the last set of questions and match your total "true" answers to the key below.

0-3 Your inner diva is in there – sadly you have not found her yet! But do not despair. Keep reading the book to find your inner diva!

4-6 Good news! You've begun to hear the whispers of your inner diva. But you are a long way from knowing your inner diva. To continue on the journey you need to continue to read the book for clues for the journey.

7-9 Great news! You have found your inner diva. But she is not free yet to empower you to be and do all you could once she is unleashed. To get to that highest level - you need to read the book and maximize your diva potential.

10 Wow! You have found your inner diva! You are someone who has heard and understood the inner voice that can transform your life and your world. To understand more about how to unleash your inner diva, see all the diva types, be able to mentor others and so much more - you need to keep reading the book.

Discovering Your Inner Diva

So what are the steps to find this elusive and mysterious essence of being a fulfilled woman?

The good news is that you can discover your inner diva. It is not one of those challenges that only a few people can do. This is not like sorting the colors on a Rubik's Cube®. It is not like assembling the furniture just bought from IKEA®. It is not like understanding the infield fly rule in baseball or why guys love watching football and hockey. It is certainly easier for most women than finding your G-spot! In fact, the process of discovering your inner diva may help you discover your G-spot... but I digress.

Here are some of the steps on the journey that will lead you to the signs that you are looking to discover. Follow the clues. Examine the trail. Look for hints. Each of us is unique and so your path to discovering your inner diva will be as individual and special as you are. You may find yourself circling over and over the same ground for a while – that's OK. Each step you take is part of the journey – even when you are covering the same ground. That is because this is not a journey to a far away place. This is not a journey away from yourself. This is a journey into the real you. The following are some of the places each woman must visit to discover her inner diva. We'll look at the need to meditate, listen, ask, watch, relax, reflect and test.

Meditate

Each of us needs to quiet ourselves from the busy and demanding world that makes up our everyday lives. That means we have to find a quiet time and a quiet place for us to withdraw from the noise. Your meditation may involve silence. Others use music or art. Some will read. Others will spend time by a river or lake or the ocean where the sounds of water take us away. For others their refuge will be in a forest or a meadow or country road where we can begin again to live in the moment. Whatever it is - it always involves stopping the rush and momentum of your day and choosing to take time out.

Listen

If you have yet to discover your inner diva – the good news is that she is calling you. It may seem like a noise, an echo or some faint distant sound. As you come closer the sound becomes clearer. Soon you begin to hear her as a voice inside. It takes time to understand what she is saying. It begins with words that sound garbled and strange. But as time passes, the words become clearer. Then it happens. You hear this voice clearly and you are enchanted. The magic has begun!

Ask

We can learn from others along the way who have connected to their inner diva. Ask them what it was that they learned on their quest already. The paths will be different since they are not us but they may be able to share some of how they learned to recognize the signs and clues along the way. Find some diva mentors – those who have connected to their inner diva and learn from them.

Watch

Watch for opportunities that come your way to express yourself. This is very important for younger people. Just as in school we can take a variety of subjects to begin to discover what we love – the same is true on your diva quest. Look for places where you can begin to test your interests. Find out what kinds of experiences bring you a deeper joy and satisfaction – not just stimulation. As you feel the contentment and sense of well-being that comes from when we are in our "diva zone" – seek more of those opportunities. Find time to do more of what you love!

Relax

Our fast paced life robs us not only of time to ourselves but even remembering how to relax. Even when we are sitting down – we may be too exhausted to actually relax. We need to learn again how to breathe and to let our body return to the ideals we enjoyed as children. It is no wonder that there is now a whole industry on relaxation therapy.

Reflect

Just as we need to take time to meditate – we also need to take time to reflect. As we go through our day – pause to actively think about what has happened to you. Bring perspective to those pieces of your daily puzzle. What did you learn from those experiences? How did you feel as you were in the middle of those moments? Learn through reflection.

Test

If your activity involves others – get some feedback from some trusted friends. Test how you think an event or your expression of yourself went. Let them give you their perspective. You have probably noticed others in your life or on the world's stage where they have expressed their inner diva. Others can recognize when something special is happening. Get feedback from your friends on times when you feel you've connected to the magic of your inner diva and see what they think. This will not replace your personal awareness of how the quest is going but often good friends will see it happening too.

Before long you will find that your inner diva has a name. You will be able to describe the special passion that you have for doing something or being something unique.

Knowing that your inner diva is there – but how do you release your inner diva from that dark and mysterious place deep within us?

Diva Passion Meter Quiz

Take this Diva Passion Meter Quiz to see what level of passion you have reached with your inner diva. Count how many of the following statements are true for you right now. The score key to interpret your results will follow. Total your score from 0-10.

- [ ] I love to start my day.
- [ ] I make a difference in my world.
- [ ] I am a person with great energy.
- [ ] I never give up.
- [ ] I am confident in what I like to do.
- [ ] I do not avoid problems – I solve them.
- [ ] I love to celebrate the success of others.
- [ ] I feel great about my future.
- [ ] I love to learn.
- [ ] I love to give to others.

What Was Your Diva Passion Score?

Take your total score from the last set of questions and match your total "true" answers to the key below.

0-3   Stone cold – your inner diva is on ice! But that is not the end of the story. You can thaw out that reservoir of dreams and passion you have been given by connecting to your inner diva. It is not only possible to do – you can do it! Get the most out of your life. Read on!

4-6   You are getting warmer! You're on your way to becoming someone who has looked deeply into yourself and found that special resource called your inner diva. But don't stop there! You can start to celebrate and enjoy the best in life as you take the next steps. To continue on the journey you need to read the rest of this book.

7-9   You are hot! You have found your inner diva and things are happening for you. You are confident about yourself and your world. Your future is bright! But to get to that highest level - you need to keep reading the book.

10   You're on fire! You are not just celebrating your inner diva – you're having a party! You understand the meaning of finding and unleashing your inner diva. You are ready to take on the challenges and opportunities of your life. What an exciting place for you to be in your life journey! To learn more about how to maximize your diva energy and connect to other kinds of divas out there – the rest of the book awaits!

Diva Power & Passion

Just as when you are developing your ability in a sport or a skill – we can measure progress. The early awkward experiences where we feel like we'll never make all these different tasks work together are gradually replaced by a higher and higher level of confidence and competence. Do you remember learning to ride your first bike? It was wobbly. Someone was probably holding you to help you balance. You wondered how you would ever stay up much less make the bike move down the street.

But then it started to happen. Before long – you were confidently breezing down the road and enjoying the feeling of the wind flowing past your face and through your hair. It was wonderful!

The same experience is true when it comes to releasing our inner diva. Once we have found her and begun to connect with her – then we need to release her through us into our world. How that happens is different for all of us. But it will not happen until we have included the following big ideas into who we are: risk, energize, enthuse and engage.

Risk

Many people miss out on some of the most important and special experiences of their life because they are afraid to take the risk. It might be a fear of failure, a fear of the unknown or a fear of change that keeps you frozen in your present unfulfilled moment. Like jumping off a diving board – we can close our eyes and hope for the best or keep our eyes wide open. To quest is to risk. You must choose to take the risk in order to grow and develop as a person. Take a chance on you!

Energize

Energy is released when there is some form of action or friction. That's true whether it is a nuclear reaction or exploding dynamite or wood burning or turbines moving as water rushes over Niagara Falls. Energy often comes from dealing with forces that seem greater than ourselves. But it is energy that brings us so many possibilities. We must engage with forces greater than ourselves to truly experience the full range of possibilities. For some people that is a natural spirituality while for others it is a personal faith. But our true energy is a gift given to us.

Enthuse

Most people do not allow themselves to get excited about life. It is all about following the same routines. Go along and be like everyone else. Do not stand out by having some oomph! Would people look at me funny if I choose to be enthusiastic about something? Does this make me hold back? The word enthuse traces its roots back to the Greek language en = in and theos = god. So enthusiasm is really allowing our God-given inspiration and emotions out into something special in life. Allowing ourselves to be enthusiastic may take some practice. But don't feel bad about that - sports teams need stadiums full of people and cheerleaders to get enthused to get to the top of their game! It begins by acknowledging that it is OK to be enthused!

Engage

Whatever your opportunity is you must choose to engage. It is different to just "be" somewhere or "do" something and really connecting to the place or activity by choosing to fully engage yourself. Most people spend their life like those cardboard standees that we see in grocery stores or movie theaters. It looks like the person is there but when you look at them from the side - you can see that they are not really there. To discover your inner diva - you have to give yourself to the experience and not hold back.

Women who have found and released their inner diva are passionate people. They have renewed their zest for life. It is especially true in the particular diva area where they excel. But it overflows into all of their life experiences. Like breathing the sea air or the inhaling the soft breeze in a meadow – everything they do is enhanced by their diva passions. They live life at a higher level. They have a confidence and power that transforms every part of their life experience because they know who they really are. Their gift is now on fire – kindling and warming all those around them. They have changed their world because they are changed.

The more passionate the diva – the more dynamic their world becomes. No matter who they are, where they live or whatever else makes up their daily routine – it is changed forever. Wow!

Diva Passion Meter Quiz

What Is Your Diva Type? This quiz will be a way to begin identifying which one is most like you. There are five main diva types. Do you know which one is you? On a piece of paper, write down 1-24. Then put a T beside each number that is true of you. The score key to interpret your results will follow.

1. I enjoy persuading others.
2. My home is a place friends come in good times or bad.
3. I need more time to be alone.
4. I enjoy having people visit at my place.
5. I am energized whenever I am in a group.
6. I love to read books, listen to music or walk by myself.
7. I know how to use personal power effectively.
8. Others ask me to help them organize events.
9. I have or want to start my own business.
10. I am always redecorating my home – even if it's only in my mind.
11. I am delighted to paint, sculpt, do crafts or other visual arts.
12. I do not like being alone.
13. I am inspired to hear or see what others have created.
14. I know most of the people in my neighborhood.
15. People always want to be around me.
16. I think that the role of government is very important.
17. I am at my best when I am with others.
18. I like earning money.
19. I love to prepare food for others and see them enjoy my cooking.
20. I enjoy my family times most of all.
21. I have made it a priority to develop my spiritual self.
22. I find satisfaction organizing social events.
23. I love to perform music or perform on stage.
24. I like being in the business world.

Now take your answers that you wrote down and match the question numbers to the letters on the grid below. For example, if you answered True for Question 1 – circle the A beside it. Do this for all the questions then total up each column to see how many A B C and Ds you have.

QUESTION	A	B	C	D
1	T			
2		T		
3			T	
4		T		
5				T
6			T	
7	T			
8				T
9	T			
10		T		
11			T	
12				T
13			T	
14		T		
15				T
16	T			
17				T
18	T			
19		T		
20		T		
21			T	
22				T
23			T	
24	T			
TOTALS				

If you have the most "T's" in the A column – you are a Business Diva! The business diva loves to be at the center of business life whether it is on Wall Street, Bay Street or Main Street. It does not matter what the business challenge is – she is raring to go because she knows she can compete with anyone – anytime. This is not arrogance – it comes from a clear awareness of who she is. Within the business diva group are the corporate diva, the entrepreneur diva, the sales diva and the government diva. To understand more about how to unleash your inner diva, detailed descriptions of the diva types and so much more – you need to read the next chapter in this book.

If you have the most "T's" in the B column – you are a Domestic Diva! The domestic diva finds her passions for life expressed in the context of her home and family. Nothing gives her more joy than see her surroundings and those she loves in a functioning, nurturing and positive environment. Within the domestic diva group are the cooking diva, the decorating diva, the family diva, the entertaining diva and the neighborhood diva. To understand more about how to unleash your inner diva, detailed descriptions of the diva types and so much more – read on!

If you have the most "T's" in the C column – you are a Creative Diva! The creative diva is the most spiritually attuned diva in our group. She is in touch with the creative impulses and passions that run deep within herself but have their source in the inspirational gifts that she has received. Within the creative diva group are artistic divas, musical divas, language divas, drama divas and spiritual divas. To understand more about how to unleash your inner diva, detailed descriptions of the diva types and so much more – keep reading the rest of the book.

If you have the most "T's" in the D column – you are a Social Diva! The social diva gets her energy and satisfaction from her social life outside the home. She's not a party animal but instead is someone who loves to make connections with people in a social context. Often she is the one who does the planning of the events as well because she has a keen sense of what works socially and how to help others have a great time. They also are often found in the helping professions. . To understand more about how to unleash your inner diva, detailed descriptions of the diva types and so much more - you need to keep on reading the book.

If you have the similar number of "T's" in all the columns – you are a Balanced Diva! The balanced divas should not be confused with Wonder Woman or Superwoman. It is not that they are trying to do it all but they can float comfortably between the varying demands of different parts of our diva lives. Those who have connected early with their inner diva are able to recognize and develop balance over the life experiences that time brings. The older balanced divas have a mature perspective that is not racing or panicking but is able to celebrate the moment – wherever they happen to be. It is a great gift and they are people who can teach us a great deal about being a diva. Keep reading the book to learn more.

If you have a similar number of "T's" in a couple of the columns – then you are a Blended Diva combining those Diva Types. See the descriptions above of your primary diva types and read on for more information.

Diva Types

There are many kinds of divas in the world. Here are just some of the types you can meet. Can you put any names or faces to any of these types of diva? Each of us adds our own special flair to our particular example of a type of diva. There are as many variations in any type of diva just as there are many shades of green in a forest. This variety makes our world a richer place.

It is very exciting to learn about your inner diva and to uncover the tremendous potential for peace, joy and satisfaction that comes from recognizing the gifts and passions that we all have been given. When those passions are allowed to express themselves in our lives – we find a wonder and energy that not only gets us through our days but makes our days meaningful.

Many people who face old age discover too late the importance of taking risks and investing in things that really matter. Sadly, too many look back on a life that played it safe and never took the risks of reaching out for something special from life. Discovering and using the potential that your inner diva offers you will not only change your today but your tomorrow as well.

What type of diva are you? Embrace it and grow!

THE CREATIVE DIVA

The creative diva is the most spiritually attuned diva in our group. She is in touch with the creative impulses and passions that run deep within herself but have their source in the inspirational gifts that she has received. These include the art divas, music divas, language divas, drama divas and the spiritual divas.

Art Divas

Art is one of these gifts where we have a glimpse of heaven on earth. Our artistic diva is able to use her talents and imagination to share with us the beauty and wonder of the world around us.

Think of the many expressions of this: Sculpture, painting, sketching, glass blowing, pottery, wood-burning, photography, weaving, folk art, crafts, videos, knitting, drawing, floral arrangements, embroidery, eggery, decorating, copper-tooling, sewing, jewelry, beading, stamping, scrapbooking, origami, woodworking, quilting, leather crafts and so much more.

Music Divas

Music is perhaps the place where some echoes of heaven is heard on earth. It is a language unto itself. There are so many ways for the musical diva to share her gift.

Here are just a few: Singing solos, composing songs, playing instruments, directing a choir or orchestra, harmonizing, playing by ear, having perfect pitch, teaching music to others, performing in musical theater, writing symphonies, tuning instruments and many other expressions of this beautiful area of life.

Language Divas

The language diva is able to use their gift with words to create beauty to be read or spoken. Our lives are enriched by those language divas who have connected with their talent for interpreting ideas and wonder through their words.

Here are just some of their expressions: Lyrics, poetry, dramas, stories, verse, speeches, fiction, non-fiction, television, movies, plays, novels and many other methods of creative words.

Drama Divas

The Drama diva can be part of bringing stories to life as they interpret and perform on stage, television, online, in movies and in so many other venues. Their work might be serious, fantasy, comedy, musicals or dramas. But they all include the love of sharing themselves with others.

Spiritual Divas

The spiritual diva is someone who is in touch with the faith dimension of life. They have a centered personality. They love people with an extraordinary sense of caring for others. They are attuned to their Creator. The have a great sense of personal peace and wholeness that reminds all of us of the need to see our world as part of a larger story and purpose.

The world is such a better place because of the creative divas who have released the many forms of beauty in our lives. Those who have truly found their passions and purpose in one of these creative pursuits not only give us joy but know what it means to celebrate a life well lived.

Go creative divas go!

THE DOMESTIC DIVA

The domestic diva finds her passions for life expressed in the context of her home and family. Nothing gives her more joy than to see her surroundings and those she loves in a functioning, nurturing and positive environment. She is organized even if it is organized chaos!

Within the group of domestic divas there are many domestic diva specialties. Here are just a few: the cooking diva, the decorating diva, the family diva, the entertaining diva and the neighborhood diva.

Cooking Diva

The cooking diva loves the world of food and drink. She loves learning about and experimenting with all kinds of appetizers, entrees, vegetables, baking, desserts and drinks. Sauces, spices and new combinations of taste sensations get their domestic juices flowing. They love the process of preparing food. But it is in serving the food and seeing the looks on her satisfied family and guests that brings her the greatest moments of satisfaction.

Decorating Diva

The decorating diva has a keen sense of color, style and occasion. They are able to bring together the right combinations of paint, wallpaper, furniture, textures, lighting, accents and art to make a room memorable. What makes them different from the creative diva is that their motivation is not so much creative but to make their home a special place.

Family Diva

The family diva is absorbed with the family life – and they love it! They relish the times when everyone is together and they can also be fully engaged with just one member of the family. Their house may or may not be as organized because it is centered on the family relationships. They often are able to enjoy the presence of the extended family members as visitors or even if they end up moving in due to failing health or age. The difference between the family diva and the traditional woman's role in the home is that this is not a role for her – it is her passion. She does it because she loves it and it gives her joy.

Entertaining Diva

The entertaining diva loves to be with people who visit her home. She loves to plan events and occasions when others can enjoy being with her and her family. The preparation and set-up for the meal or party is motivated by the desire to entertain others and to give them a memorable time. The ringing of the doorbell or knock at the door announces the fun has begun. She is able to make each guest feel like a king or queen as they enjoy the festivities. She enjoys knowing that her luncheon or dinner was a great success.

Neighborhood Diva

The neighborhood diva uses her home and domestic instincts to create a real sense of community in the neighborhood. She will invite neighbors over for coffee or tea. Her home is open for the neighborhood kids to enjoy with her own children. She is the first to welcome someone who has just moved into the community. When someone is elderly, sick or has suffered a loss in the neighborhood – she is there with a meal and some encouragement. She watches out for those in need and knows how to help without alienating the person or family. If you are away on vacation, she will check your mail and watch the house for you. The neighborhood diva is always the one who remembers to say goodbye when you move away. Our communities need more neighborhood divas!

SOCIAL DIVA

The social diva gets her energy and satisfaction from her social life outside the home. She's not a party animal but instead is someone who loves to make connections with people in a social context. Often she is the one who does the planning of the events as well because she has a keen sense of what works socially and how to help others have a great time.

They also are often found in the helping professions because of their great SQ – social quotient. Some people have a very high IQ – intelligence quotient and others have a high SQ which gives them the ability to perceive what's happening socially beyond what most people can. The social divas enjoy being with people. They look for opportunities to gather with people – and the bigger the gathering the better. As they are so experienced with people and social occasions they know how to plan what works well. They have been to terrible events that were poorly run. They also have been at the best in town events too. The social divas take pride in being part of pulling off a great occasion that people will talk about for years to come.

Intricate event planning that would make any other person go crazy actually stimulates the social diva. They love the challenge and will leap to any opportunity to make it possible for others to have a great time.

This group includes the gala divas, the serving divas, the culinary diva, the conversational diva, the mentoring diva.

Gala Diva

These people are the ones who run everything from the million dollar gala fundraisers or the church social. They are the ones who are always there when a funeral wake is to be held, a wedding shower is to be planned, hosting a soup kitchen or when someone is retiring.

Serving Diva

The very best of the social divas are often found in careers that are the helping professions like nurses, social workers, government and community service agencies. Some are wedding planners or coordinate sports events. In the service of others through their careers, these are the often selfless people who will always go the extra mile to take care of others – even strangers. It is part of their nature to be there for others in need whether that need is a life crisis or just the need to have a good time in what can be a difficult world.

Culinary Diva

The culinary diva knows how to use the selection, preparation and presentation of food to make others feel special. They have a growing knowledge and insight into the world of appetizers, drinks, entrees and desserts. Never content with the same old experiences – they always find a way to move their guests to a new culinary delight without making them feel like visitors to a laboratory. She can account for the wide range of taste experiences so everyone has a positive experience no matter what they are used to eating. Food, glorious food is only the beginning for her. It is how that food is prepared and presented that are also important to her – even if other's do not know all the detail and care that went into her work. She knows! Of course – if others notice and compliment her on it – she will not be disappointed…

The Conversational Diva

The best conversationalists are the social divas because they have spent so much time with others that they know so many stories to share. They are never at a loss for words – even when they are alone!

The Mentoring Diva

Many social divas also are mentors and teachers. They are the ones who carry on and then pass on the traditions and joys of our relationships for us to treasure. As people-people, they love to share who they are and understand that more than ideas need to be passed along – we share life to life. These are the ones who invest in future generations and keep alive the best of what we know and who we are.

Those social divas who have connected with their passions make a difficult and challenging world a kinder and gentler place for all of us.

THE BUSINESS DIVA

The business diva loves to be at the center of business life whether it is on Wall Street, Bay Street or Main Street. It does not matter what the business challenge is – she is raring to go because she knows she can compete with anyone – anytime. This is not arrogance or pride – it is an awareness of who she is. These are women who are assertive – a good thing. That is different from what detractors will often call them – aggressive. Assertive women do not hesitate to declare who they are and what they can do. They do not need to be aggressive to succeed. Like most women – the business diva has fought many battles to get where she is. Some of them were early stereotypes while others were outright hostility. Just as the women of World War II learned – if it needed doing and there were no men to do it – women did it and did it very well. Now the business diva is not content to be Rosie the Riveter or the secretary. The types of business divas include: the corporate diva, the entrepreneur diva, the sales diva and the government diva.

The Corporate Diva

More and more corporations have experienced women as senior executives and CEOs. To the surprise of the traditionalists – the companies do not fall apart. What a surprise! The corporate diva is using her confidence and passion to make a difference in the corner offices and boardrooms around the world as well as running the local business on Main Street in a city or town near you. Women can succeed in the corporate world because they bring a fresh new focus and ideas to the table with their special ability to give attention to details that are often missed otherwise.

The Entrepreneur Diva

Women account for a large percentage of new and small businesses today. As women gain experience, mentors and confidence – this will continue to increase. The entrepreneur diva is driving many of these new enterprises. With the courage to take the risks of beginning something new – women are creating jobs and opportunities for ownership and wealth building for themselves and for future generations.

The Sales Diva

Sales are critical to the survival and growth of any company. Without sales – where would we be? The sales diva is a growing part of the sales force who are able to not only generate more sales with women but men too. These sales divas are committed to learning and growing in their knowledge and execution of the products and services that they represent.

The Government Diva

While government is not technically business – the government divas are all business when it comes to providing leadership and perspective in their places in government. The government divas know how to be as tough as the next guy when needed but also understand that sometimes it is about understanding the problem rather than fighting for the last inch of ground. The government divas are changing the way we are governed and the way we think about government too.

THE BALANCED DIVA

Most women have some elements of different diva types already in their experience. Our experiences combined with our natural inclinations and gifts allow us to learn from other diva styles and adapt them to our life and needs. Learning is so important for us throughout our life.

You will meet some divas who have found their inner diva is one of balance. Like a liberal arts education – they draw on a wide range of knowledge and experience to be who they are. They may not be as gifted or talented in any one direction as some of the other divas but they are able to work in many different situations very comfortably. They can combine pieces of the social, creative, business and domestic divas in a centered way. We call these balanced divas.

The balanced divas should not be confused with Wonder Woman or Superwoman. It is not that they are trying to do it all but they can float comfortably between the varying demands of different parts of their diva lives. Those who have connected early with their inner diva are able to recognize and develop balance over the life experiences that time brings. The older balanced divas have a mature perspective that is not racing or panicking but is able to celebrate the moment – wherever they happen to be. It is a great gift and they are people who can teach us a great deal about being a diva.

Curiouser and Curiouser

Divas are curious people. There are many ways you can take that. We are a strange bunch! Divas get to be divas because they figure themselves out. That gives them an advantage when it comes to figuring life out too. That's part of what gives us the edge in dealing with people and challenges in our life. We are curious to learn more about who we are, the others in our life and the big wide world.

Most people have heard the phrase "lifelong learning" but we tend to equate that with taking courses at university or college. But lifelong learning is more than just taking a course – it is an attitude that we can and should keep learning! One of my roles is as an inspirational speaker and trainer. I teach a variety of topics including professional training for people who are gaining certifications or qualifications in the insurance restoration field. People in jobs that require training to keep up their certifications tend to understand the need for those courses but even they often neglect the bigger idea of lifelong learning.

Lifelong learning is about life not just our job. It is great to keep up or develop your employment skills but you are more than your job. To reach our goals to be the best we can be we need to continue our development as a person. That includes our career development but it also includes learning about our health, our relationships, our minds, and our spiritual self too. Lifelong learning trains our mental muscles.

Knowledge is power for the diva – but it is also a source of joy and balance. Celebrating art, enjoying music, reading books and watching movies all contribute to giving us more perspective about life and how we fit into it. The ability to understand a wide range of topics helps us whenever we are socializing since we can relate better to what people care about. This makes us feel more comfortable and that allows us to be confident when we are in a setting with new people.

This also will give us greater balance in our lives too. If we are all work and no play – we will soon find ourselves unfulfilled as people. That's not diva worthy!

Another advantage that we have in our time is that we can access opportunities for learning and personal development.

No surprise – but I do recommend going to seminars or workshops in a field that interests you where you can learn something new or a new way of looking at a topic. We live in an age with many great seminar speakers. If you can not attend in person you can now be virtually at the seminar through the use of videos and audio CDs. One of the latest innovations is watching seminars online. You can benefit from people speaking on a huge range of topics without ever leaving your home – or getting out of your pajamas! Information about my seminar programs at Representing All Women is available on our website: www.representingallwomen.com.

The fact that you are reading this book is a good sign! But instead of only buying books that "do something" for you – grab some time with books that are on topics that are totally "useless" to some like a book on travelling to far away places or history or biographies of someone you know very little about. Many people enjoy reading a book from a subject that they might have hated in school but now with no pressure of an exam or paper – you can enjoy learning about it again.

So while curiosity may have killed the cat – it makes you the diva!

Draw A Circle

Circles are one of those primary shapes that we learn to draw early in school. Most of us struggle to make it round but we keep trying!

If you are going to succeed as a diva you will need to have a special circle in your life. This one will not be drawn with a pencil or a pen – it will be painted with the special friends that you choose to make part of your life. These are your "inner circle" that every leader from a President of the United States to the local PTA has.

The need for an inner circle for the diva comes from the fact that when you lead or excel – it is easy to become a loner. It's often lonely at the top! Many people you know will resist your achievements or envy them when you begin to unleash your inner diva. Like lobsters in a bucket – some will try to pull you back down to where they live in their petty battles and sense of "we're all destined to be cooked" worldview.

In the outside world there are groups and individuals that will attack you like wolves. But like caribou or water buffalo, if you have friends who will form a circle with you – you can stay safe until the wolves give up.

Choose your circle of friends well. Many successful business people, celebrities or politicians will tell you that it is so important to have some friends who knew you way back then. As we become more successful – it is easy for us to wonder whether someone likes us or is hanging around because of what we have become in business or life – or whether it is because of who we are as a person.

My best friend Jennifer – a true friend to me – whether I was up or down, rich or poor, unknown or well known. She was always there for me. No matter how long we had gone without seeing each other – we picked up our relationship just where we left off – without dropping a beat. I've learned through Jennifer the value of old and faithful friends!

Too often people allow the "yessirs" to surround them. People who are hangers-on and wannabees or who want to fawn over you are easy to find. They will love to come along for the ride with you as long as you're making it happen. They'll tell you anything you want to hear and will feed your ego. But beware of these people. What they are feeding you is a diet of soda and candy floss. Live on it for very long and you will get sick. And if you ever face hard times – they'll be gone in a flash.

Some people are naturals at making friends. Other people need some help. There are many resources out there to help us learn about making and keeping friends. Observe the friendly people in your life and learn from them. The friendly people also tend to be the positive ones too. Those are the keepers who will help you grow and will have your back when troubles inevitably come.

Draw a circle of old friends and add to it people who are successful in their own world – they will understand some of what you have gone through. They also will appreciate you not just for what they can get out of you.

True friends take an investment of your time, energy and commitment over years. Being a true diva is to be centered as a person – not self-centered. The ability to make and keep friends is a sign of you being a healthy person. Start investing in those relationships today and every day! It is the diva thing to do!

Forgive To Live!

One of the ways that you can tell if someone has unleashed their inner diva is when you listen to them talk about their most difficult relationships. Everyone has relationships that are difficult, painful and disappointing. That is part of human nature – and we all spend part of our lives repairing or running from these broken relationships.

But not all relationships can be fixed. It takes two people to make a relationship work. So even if one of you works hard and is willing to do whatever it takes to keep a relationship – the other person can decide that they can not or will not make it work. You can then spend your life and energy chasing a relationship that just will not work.

When you have that kind of lost relationship – it can bring you a great deal of pain. All of us can think of situations where we did not have the kind of relationship we wished we had. This can be some of our most basic relationships like a mom or dad who were distant, dysfunctional or hurtful. If you have lost communication with a son or daughter – there is a huge hole in your life. It could be another family member, someone who was a friend, neighbor or colleague. Most painful is usually a lost love – especially if there is a divorce with all the legal wrangling involved. We end up with a long list of disappointments and hurts that accumulate over a lifetime.

You can not control what others will do with the opportunity to have a relationship with you. But what you can control is what you choose to do with any relationship – positive or negative – failed or growing. You can decide what you will do. My friend Marcia Wieder always says "Go and clean it up!"

I am a great believer in staying positive and part of the way you stay positive is to be around positive, growing people. That is a choice you can make.

But sometimes our lives include negative people in our workplace, our neighborhood and even our family. That's where we can and should choose to be a positive person – no matter how negative other people behave around us. That's part of being us.

When you do look at these hurtful moments in a good relationship or the typical moments in a toxic relationship – how do you keep going? How do you not get stuck in the quicksand of those negative feelings in the pit of your stomach every time someone mentions their name or when you see them coming down the hall?

The answer is to forgive.

I learned about the power of forgiveness from Grant, my friend. This is a theme you can hear from Tony Robbins and many others too. Like most people, I had thought about forgiveness as something others need me to do for them. The truth is that forgiveness is something I need for myself and for me to have a positive life.

When someone hurts or disappoints us – we have the choice to forgive them or to hold it against them. Most people have long lists of painful memories that they can recite about all the things others did to them. These are like chains that wrap around you again and again until you feel so heavy that your spirit could not soar – even in the best of times. All of the positive energy that you could have spent on making life better for you and those in your life is drained. This bitterness becomes like kryptonite is to Superman… no energy and no super powers. You can never be the strong, passionate person you could be because you are thinking about the negative things happening in your life.

The other strange but true part of this idea of forgiveness is that most people who have offended us do not even remember doing it. Maybe it was not a big deal to them – while it was huge to us. Perhaps they were insensitive when they did whatever it was that hurt us. If so, why would we then be surprised that an insensitive person didn't notice they were insensitive? It could be that we were being overly-sensitive at the time. Maybe we misunderstood what they were saying or doing. The reality is that we could be carrying around a pop-up file of terrible things a person did to us that is zapping our energy and creativity every day – and they don't even know it!

I'm not talking here about whether a person should be charged with a crime or sued. This is not about the legal consequences of someone injuring us or doing something illegal. But even where a crime has been committed – there is a good reason for us to choose to forgive the other person – regardless of whether they are charged with a crime or sued for some wrongdoing against us.

One of the best examples of this was Pope John Paul II and Mehmet Ali Agca who shot the Pope in May 1981. In December 1983, it was the Pope who visited his would be assassin in his jail cell and offered him his forgiveness. The Pope was not making a legal judgment – Agca still went to jail for life (though was later pardoned by the Italian government in 2000 at the Pope's request). But the act of choosing to forgive gave the Pope the freedom to move on with his life.

By choosing to forgive – we set ourselves free from the emotional bondage that can make and keep us bitter for the rest of our lives. Does this make us weak doormats inviting everyone to walk all over us? Not at all! In fact, it makes us stronger because we choose to forgive and that gives us a more positive future.

Is forgiving someone who has hurt us easy? Not at first. It may seem like you will never be able to forgive someone else. But like many things in life – it takes some practice. Once you start practicing forgiveness the possibility of forgetting those offenses starts to happen. That's when the magic begins!

But like other important parts of unleashing your inner diva – only you can choose to make your life better and more meaningful.

Shaboo On!

Being a diva means being a social person. While you may not be a social diva - all divas who have discovered their inner power ultimately connect to people. You will not have much of an impact on the world if you are an island. Perhaps you are one of those people who feel uncomfortable in social situations like a party or another social event. What do I say? What do I do? How do I fit in and still be me?

I love the word "shaboo" for this. Shaboo is one of those neat sounding words that has some energy to it. Just like the word "buzz" or "crash" it is a word that gets you going. It has power and life. For those of you not familiar with the term - shaboo means a party or gathering or social event that has a special quality that puts it above the typical similar event. There are parties - and then there are shaboo parties. There are weddings. Then there are shaboo weddings. There are retirements and then there are shaboo retirements. There are funeral wakes - and then there are shaboo funerals. The shaboo events always have that special magic usually created by the planning and energy that goes into taking a routine event and making it a cut above. Sometimes it is the chemistry of those hosting or creating the event. Other times it is how the event is staged or pulled off that makes everyone who is there feel like they have been at something extraordinary and that they themselves are special.

In its first uses, the term was associated with gatherings of nurses in Canada. Strange since you don't think of nurses as being people who know how to party - and yet the good nurses have to have very special social skills to pull together everything that happens every day as a nurse. Between the extras required for great patient care and the ability to work with physicians, staff, families and the many others who are part of the hospital scene - it is no wonder that they understand how to make a social gathering awesome.

So how do you use social occasions as part of your personal growth and development as a diva?

Go!

If you are like most people – it is easy to pass on weddings, funerals, retirement dinners and community fundraising events. It feels like jury duty. You hope you are never invited… and if you do get invited – you hope you can get out of it!

But like jury duty or teaching or giving of yourself – you gain much more when you give of your time and social commitment by participating. Going to social events teaches you about how people think and behave. It helps your social intelligence – your SQ – social quotient instead of your IQ – intelligence quotient. Divas who are reaching their goals and dreams in life understand how to get along with people. And there is no way to get along with people unless you understand them. Social occasions like a shaboo are where you can get some of your social education.

This is nothing new really. People who have needed or wanted to get ahead socially always took time to learn about how to get along. That's why for generations the upper classes in Britain or the US or any culture made sure their children learned about the social world through boarding schools, finishing schools – the right schools. All of this was to enhance their ability to make it in the social tests you would later face in business or government or just being Lords and Ladies. Looking back we now look at this as something stiff and limiting. But what it actually did was give people confidence that they would know how to behave (and just as important – what others were thinking, feeling and doing) in any social setting.

This did two things. It prevented you from embarrassing yourself and weakening your position. It also gave you the confidence to put yourself forward into a social setting because you knew how to do it.

It is no different than learning the dance moves so that when you are out on the dance floor – you know what to do – whether it is a minuet, a jitterbug, square dancing, the twist or hip-hop. You can see the social dance anytime you watch world leaders at state occasions or even a press conference. There is a choreographed set of moves that allows everyone to relax a bit since they know what they and others are going to do.

It is the same as choosing the right schools. Going to the right schools announced something about you without you ever having to say a word. It also made you social connections that would later help you in your social, business and professional worlds. And if the right school you attended happened to be one of the best schools – you even received an education too!

So perhaps you are one of the people whose parents dragged them to every kind of social event. Maybe you came from a large family and there was always a bunch of family events every year from showers for a newborn to a family reunion to a big birthday, a retirement or finally a funeral. You were given a great social gift. You have already learned a great deal about people in a social setting.

Some of you were people who were taken to social events in your hometown – from the county fair or the local play or maybe the symphony. All those experiences in your past help you even if you don't realize it. It is all part of the social information and experience that helps us know what is going on in our social world.

If you did not have these experiences – go get them! Get involved in groups or events in your community. If you are a person of faith – go to church, synagogue or your mosque. Are you in a small community? Another person willing to get involved with others will make a huge difference. Volunteer somewhere. Do something with other people where you're giving.

You don't have to do everything – but do something.

Then do what you can to take that party or event to make it into a shaboo. What is the extra something that you or that group can do to make that event special and memorable rather than just another formality. As has been said by my friend Grant in his friendship seminars, "Make memories for others today and you'll make joy for your old age."

Be alert to what you are seeing around you. Listen to others as they talk about themselves. Ask them questions about their life stories. Invite people to share their experiences and you will grow stronger and more confident socially because each new experience will seem familiar – because you have already been there in some other way.

Getting out into social events will help build your self-esteem – you will feel better about yourself when you're sharing and contributing to others. You'll also learn about yourself and be more comfortable in every other social engagement you'll encounter as you unleash your inner diva.

Hire The Coach

Great teams and great players in any sport can point to a particular coach that made a difference for them. Maybe it was the one-on-one coach in gymnastics or sometimes the coach working with the whole basketball or football team. But something special happens between that coach and the players on that team. They are able to do some magic that not only teaches the skills of the sport – but releases that special inner potential too.

Many people benefit from coaching in life and business as well. A life coach or an executive coach (for those in leadership or business or in government) – can make a real difference in your potential for success. Let's be clear about coaching. Coaches do not solve problems – they assist us in clarifying our plan moving forward in the direction we have chosen to go.

Coaches are different than counselors who are exploring our past to understand our present - they are not therapists and do not take their place if you have past issues that need therapy. Nor are they just cheerleaders who celebrate our victories. Coaches help you understand what is happening in your life right now and do a combination of challenging and encouraging you to help you achieve your best as a person.

The best coaches are those who help you through listening, reflection, perspective, balance and encouragement. They are also concerned about your whole person – including the spiritual side of life – not just how to make the next buck or solve the next problem. They will take time to understand who you are, what your goals and objectives are and then how you want to get there. They walk alongside you on your journey and will provide you with an objective voice when so many around you may be silent or just telling you what you want to hear.

I have had a coach for many years. My relationship with my coach was founded through one of my experiences with motivational speaker Tony Robbins. Her name is Elisa Palombi at www.biglifegroup.com. She is a master coach and her coaching has been invaluable to me.

Get a coach who will help you reach and keep your full potential as a person. You are worth it! As a Dream Coach, I understand the power that excellent coaching can bring to people once they recognize their true potential. I enjoy the process of encouraging and motivating others one on one – just as I find great satisfaction when I speak to groups.

Take Care of You!

One of the side-effects of the low self-esteem that many women experience is that they tend to ignore their own health concerns. It is as if we do not really matter enough to make our personal wellness a priority. We can get caught in the familiar trap of taking care of everyone except us. We have a tradition over many generations of sacrificing ourselves to the needs of others. This is not all bad – it is part of why we have such an important role in the life of our families, our communities and our world at large.

But as you think it through – we not only deserve to take care of our health – we need to be healthy. If your motivation is taking care of others in your life – you'll never be able to do this is you are not well. We have also learned the importance of modeling for our children. What does it teach our sons and daughters if mom does not take care of her health?

Taking charge of our health is our responsibility. We can not depend on anyone else to care about our healthcare if we do not. No doctor, HMO, healthcare plan, government or anyone else will take care of us if we do not take care of ourselves.

Many of us have our struggles. For some of us it is the persistent battle with weight. For others it might be smoking. You may have a chronic illness like diabetes or arthritis. Many women have carpal tunnel syndrome or other repetitive strain injuries associated with our jobs. Menopause and peri-menopause seem to arrive way too soon for all of us. We all want to fight the aging process. Depression is a fact of life for many women. Some women worry about breast cancer.

For many years I've been fortunate to have a health coach Doug Caporrino. Doug has had to approach my health and fitness first from the 6 inches in between my ears. His philosophy is you cannot get the body to go where you want it to, until you get the mind to go there first. He told me that we need to strip ourselves of all our beliefs that do you absolutely no good and create new and healthy ones. Thinking, sleeping and eating your way into a lifestyle is the only way to succeed. Diets and quick fixes don't work. A little focus and discipline go a long way to achieving success. Doug can be reached at www.resultsthruresearch.com

What can you do? A diva takes charge of what you can control and makes choices to give you the greatest level of health and vitality possible. If you want to live life to the full – you have to make healthy choices to be your best.

Like so many areas of life – taking charge starts with learning.

We live in a time when more research and new understandings of our health is happening than in any time in history. More and more this knowledge is translated into understandable language and steps we can choose to take to be well. While medical information on the internet always needs to be verified and we always should consult our healthcare professionals about what is best for us in particular – the World Wide Web is a great place to begin learning. There are many very helpful physician websites where you can learn from a physician who specializes in an area of healthcare. It helps you to have the questions to discuss with your doctor and other professionals in your life.

Let me share with you some topics for you to explore. Check out these resources and with your doctor – see if it could help you to become healthier and more vital as a person.

Detoxing our bodies. In an ideal world we could detox ourselves. However times have changed. Our bodies are under-worked and over performed. This has been attributed to the overload of chemicals in our bodies that we get from the foods we eat, primarily herbicides, fungicides, and pesticides. You see the food we eat today is not as "rich" in nutrients as they used to be which is a major reason we have to use supplements.

Hormones have long been ignored by our medical community with women being written off as hormonal, just having PMS or being menopausal. Even the word hysterical has its roots in the female anatomy. Many pieces of the glass ceiling intended to keep women from being Commander-in-Chief of the country or a company or elsewhere is based on the often whispered fear that hormonal imbalance will create a bad decision and if you were a woman President of the United States – you might blow up the world. We all know about the many changes that hormones bring into our lives. The good news is that there is an increased understanding of the importance of hormones and new ways to allow our hormones to play a positive part in our lives.

Developments have also become available in laser treatments or low level light therapy. Light therapy is the application of light energy to the skin for therapeutic benefits. It is a natural photobiochemical reaction similar to the process of plant photosynthesis. NASA's space program has proven that LED light therapy (near-infrared) promotes healing and human tissue growth. The energy delivered by the Light Emitting Diodes (LED's) has been shown to enhance cellular metabolism, accelerate the repair and replenishment of damaged skin cells, as well as stimulate growth.

Hormones are important to all women no matter whether you are beginning puberty, are in child-bearing years, entering perimenopause or are in menopause. For generations, it was something most people and even most physicians did not address well with their patients. You may have heard about Suzanne Somers talking about bio-identical hormones. This is a new area where positive things are happening.

One of the best recognized doctors I know of is Dr. Christine Northrup, M.D. Internationally known for her empowering approach to women's health and wellness, Dr. Northrup is a leading proponent of medicine and healing that acknowledges the unity of the mind and body, as well as the powerful role of the human spirit in creating health. Dr. Northrup has dedicated her lifework to helping women (and the men who love them) learn how to flourish on all levels by creating health, prosperity, and pleasure in their lives. She says, "I've spent the first half of my life studying and footnoting everything that can go wrong with the female body—and figuring out how to fix it. I'm dedicating the second half of my life to illuminating everything that can go right with the female body, including teaching women how to truly flourish." www.drnorthrup.com

Many women experience pain. It can rob us of our energy, our drive and even our sleep. It can bring on limitations in our body and depression in our soul. It can turn a positive person into someone who is depending on pain killers or even worse – alcohol – to get through the day. After speaking with my health coach Doug, he mentioned that the pain we feel is resulting from inflammation. More often then not it is an imbalance of Omega 3's, 6's and 9's.

We can reverse many pain conditions and delay the onset of many others by taking care of ourselves. There are also some great supplements to consider with your healthcare professionals. For reduced inflammation that is often associated with pain conditions there are pharmaceutical grade Omega 3's in highly refined fish oils that also have studies to show benefits to other health conditions. www.seeyourselfwell.com

Anti-aging is an area of healthcare that is growing dramatically as the population ages. We all want to put off the inevitable losses of energy and health that comes with the aging process. One of the new areas to explore is ORAC which stands for Oxygen Radical Absorbance Capacity. ORAC liquid vitamin supplements are a powerful way to help your body fight off the aging process. Learn more about this at www.oracpremium.com

The Seven Vitalities are a wonderful presentation by Toronto pharmacist David Garshowitz on balancing some of the essentials of life. He talks about the need to eat well, sleep well, have regular bowel movements to eliminate the toxins in our bodies, to use supplements that compensate for our missing vitamins and minerals, to have sufficient exercise, to have an attitude of congeniality and to embrace spirituality in your life. The presence of these seven vitalities will help us to be more effective and successful in all we do. For more information on this visit www.yorkdownsrx.com

Do you want to release your inner diva? Be healthy! Be well! Keep learning about your health and take charge of your long-term wellness.

Lost In The Clouds

I live in a part of North America where we seem to get all four seasons in a big way. When it is winter – we get the ice, sleet, damp bone chilling cold and piles of snow. Our springs can see our world of white snow with black and bare trees transform into beautiful greens that burst from the buds into leaves. The grass and fields come alive. The summer gives us intense heat and the joys of the beautiful world around us. When it is Autumn's turn – nature paints our leaves with bright reds, yellows and oranges as if to have a party before winter comes.

Whatever the seasons – we can be sure to have clouds here. Some will be the light and fluffy clouds that float by on a summer afternoon – a change of scene on a beautiful day. Others will be a dark and menacing character rising in the distance foretelling a thunderstorm is coming. Once the fall is here – we might have those heavy banks of dark clouds – where everyone looks and says that it might be snow coming. A spring shower might come with some clouds that are scooting over the fields on a day in May.

The most difficult clouds come when they are not away up there – but when they come right down to where we walk and talk. The torrential rain, the snow squalls or the dense fog – these are times when our weather is all cloud.

If you are a pilot surrounded by clouds – you can no longer rely on your ability to see the horizon or the sky above or the land below. You must rely on your instruments to find your way through the clouds.

Like many women of my generation, I grew up in a place where it was difficult to see the horizon – or any blue sky ahead. It was not just our head that was in the clouds – we were in the driving storm that comes from the challenges of a dysfunctional home life, media that defines physical perfection as the norm we should seek and glass ceilings that begin in our heads long before we enter the workplace.

My future looked like so many of you – it seemed very cloudy.

I was one of those people who seemed to have everything going against me. I grew up in a dysfunctional home-not something so unusual for my generation. I have a younger sister and we grew up going to a school system with lots of rules and not many friends. I wasn't very popular and I had my fair share of being picked on by the other kids.

As much as I did not have many of the things that my fellow students had - I was missing something even more important. I did not feel good about myself as a person.

Like many children from difficult backgrounds I still had dreams. I dreamed that I could be somebody. I dreamed that I could have a nice house. I dreamed that I would have a great job. I dreamed that I could have enough money to buy the things I wanted. I dreamed that I could have a happy life. If you knew me back then, you might think that I didn't have dreams - you would think that I had a vivid imagination! How could someone with my story have a happy and exciting future?

But the dreams that I had would not let me go. They grew stronger and bigger until I began to believe that I could do some great things. These big, big dreams kept me floating above many of the painful moments of my life.

By the time I got to high school I began to believe that some great things could happen to me. I understood that these dreams would not happen on their own but that it would take hard work by me and a commitment to setting and reaching my goals. It is as if my dreams were the fuel that kept me going during times when the there was disappointments and setbacks.

Many people believe that dreams are just like a fluffy pillow. You can sleep your life away on it. Dreams are nice to look at but they really are not very important or strong – they are just a distraction. Dreams are not to be confused with a fantasy – you can do something about your dreams. A fantasy is always still a fantasy.

But I have come to learn the dreams are the most powerful part of the human experience. Through our dreams and hopes we can leave where we are and create something new and different that can change us and can change our world!

Maybe you are one of those people who have the same dreams for a better life and a better you. Maybe you have dreams that shout at you and will not let you ignore them. Maybe you have dreams that have been forced into a very small place and they can only whisper to you right now. Maybe your life has been so difficult that you feel like you don't have any dreams left.

Let me help you find your dreams and understand what they're saying to you. Together we can have it all.

So no matter whether the clouds in your life have you surrounded in a fog, hurricane or snowstorm – do not give up! Your blue sky is just a small dream away. Life challenges our dreams. Whatever negative life experiences you encounter are just a test of our commitment to our dreams.

Call me a dreamer! You bet I am! Let's do some dreaming together!

Dream On!

The funny thing about most dreams is that they don't just happen on their own. Even when we can see them clearly and describe them easily – we usually have to do something about it.

Think of all the fairy tales and stories that have been told over the centuries. Most of the great adventures may have begun with someone just minding their own business but somewhere in the tale – they had to make a choice. The good that comes to the characters in the story don't just happen because you were there. You have to engage the adventure for it to be your own. Many people probably saw an adventure coming and went back into their house and bolted the door. We don't know about these people. The ones you know in fairy tales and in life are the ones who chose the adventure.

That is very true for us as well. Having a dream is great. Choosing to do something with your dream is essential. Whatever you understand your dreams to be right now – your dreams involve choices too. No matter where you are in your life – you can choose to start your adventure today.

My very good friend and seminar speaker is Marcia Wieder. At her seminars she talks about dreams. She talks about two types of dreams. There are the dreams we have for our life and then there are the dreams that life has for you. It is so important to know the difference. People live their life with one foot in reality and one foot in the doubt. She works with us to move one foot from doubt to the dream with our other firmly in reality. The doubter wants to test "our commitment to the dream." The realist wants to know "what the plan is?" www.dreamcoach.com

What are your dreams? Is it to be financially secure? Is it to start a new career? Do you want to go back to school? Are you looking for a positive, lifelong relationship? Do you want to start your own business? Is it politics? Perhaps you want to start an organization that will make a difference? Are you someone who has a talent like singing or art that is waiting to be explored?

Everyone's dream is different – and these dreams transform over our lifetime.

Sometimes it seems easier for us just to give up and let the river of life float us along wherever it wants to go. That does seem like an easier choice at the beginning. There's no struggle. No hard thinking or life-changing work. We just give life permission to do whatever it wants.

But as you go through life you quickly learn that life often becomes a very unfulfilling and boring experience if we decide to just be passive and let it all go. Just like the chick hatching – we have to do our part to break out of our beginning – whether it was comfortable or not – in order to experience the possibilities of the wide world.

The first thing I had to do was to bring my dream into focus. What was my dream? What was that "something" that I just have to do? What is that big idea or place that I just must get to – no matter how difficult it will be?

As you can answer that question, you will begin to see what your dream – and you – can become.

Maybe you are one of those people who do not have any dreams left. Perhaps your life seems so desert dry that you feel like all your dreams have evaporated over a lifetime of disappointment or discouragement.

Let me reassure you. Your dream is still out there. It is still alive. It may need some watering and refreshment. It may be require that you may need to take that one more chance of being hurt and disappointed to let the possibility of your life happen. But IT IS THERE!

If you are someone who is hunting for that lost dream – call out to it. Find a quiet place and a quiet moment. Take the risk. Allow your mind to search for it. Don't listen to the negative voices around you that say your dream is just a fantasy. If you have had a lifetime of people saying you can't – perhaps the loudest voice is the one in your head saying that you can't have your dream. Maybe you've been told – and you believe the lie – that you are not worth it.

Find a new voice. You are worth it. You can reach your dream. Invite a friend to help you hunt for this important part of your life. Surround yourself with people who will believe in you and your dream. Share your dreams. By declaring your dream you might actually decide to do something about it! Once you have rediscovered your dream – you'll never be the same again!

It's Great To Be You!

Self-esteem is one of the most neglected areas of life for most women. Many women begin their lives feeling badly about who they are, how they look and what they can do. Self-esteem coach and educator Joan Komer (www.drkomer.com) is one of the people who has challenged women to face the challenges of feeling good about who you are no matter what stage of life we are at today. So many people carry the negative messages throughout their lifetime robbing them of not only their joy but also their dreams.

But you have a choice. You are worth it! You are special! You are important not just for what you do but for who you are!!!

The most interesting people you will ever meet are not the people who are just floating down the river of life. They may be able to tell you how predictable and safe their life is. Sadly, they get so used to the quiet and peaceful flow that they grumble at the smallest waves or ripples that might come their way. But you have to wonder if they are really awake or whether they have just been lulled into a state where they no longer sense anything other than the steady drift down their life's course. They coast and drift only to awaken at the end of their life story with a dreadful sense that it has all passed them by. They ask why they didn't take some risks. They wonder why they settled for the easy experience. As my mom used to tell me, "Don't blink and be fifty kiddo and wish that you never tried."

Don't be that kind of drifter. Be one of those people who want more out of life than just the predictable and safe – our dreams are there. Do you want to be inspired about your dreams? Talk to some other dreamers who are truly awake. Give yourself permission to dream on!

Make Your Dreams Come True

For me to realize my dreams, I had to go on a passion quest. I had to become passionate about finding and holding on to my dreams.

There were three things that I had to do in making my dreams come true.

Clarify Your Dream

The first was to be clear about what my dream was. In my case, my dream of a successful business was something I knew would be a challenge. But I began to visualize what that would look like. My life would involve creating and running a business where I could realize the personal satisfaction of achieving financial independence and a sense of making a difference in the world through my work.

All of this required a very basic decision. I was going for it. How I would get there would need to be worked out. But I knew which way I was heading at last. It is never too late to start. Make the choice to follow your dream!

Choose To Believe In Your Dream

The second thing is a big challenge for people who have grown up in negative environments or who have experienced many disappointments in their life. How do you believe that what you do not have right now can come true for you? One of the best ways I know is to talk to (and especially listen to!!) people who have made their dream come true. You will find it encouraging as you come to learn that all kinds of people with seemingly insurmountable challenges still reached their goals.

Usually they were knocked off course a few times – I certainly have been – but they kept going. We live in a time that celebrates success but in order to achieve success in any field we have to experience some failures too. We can learn so much more from those failures that they become a positive source for us rather than a negative.

The great Walt Disney who would bring so many magical moments through his movies, television, music and his theme parks went bankrupt. He was left with his suitcase and $20 as he went west to Hollywood. He did not allow his "wish on a star" to go out even when it seemed really dark. Sometimes we can see those stars even better when we're facing a dark time.

You have to believe that if you are willing to work hard and smart toward your goal – and you will get there!

Take Massive And Immediate Action On Your Dream

The third idea is that you have to take massive and immediate action. It's important to know what your dream is and then to believe in it. Have you ever thought of a better way to do something? Maybe there is something that you know could work well if it was done a different way. How many people have come up with a great invention – only to read about the person who actually did something with it? While most people look at an invention that has made someone fabulously wealthy and say, "Why didn't I think of that?" pity the person who thought of it and never did anything about it! Who has fulfilled their dream and who is left to play "if only" for the rest of their life. But if you never take action – it will always be one of those great ideas that someone else did.

Usually the dream will take some time to achieve. I am a great believer in setting and following goals. That helps me to take the big dream and break down the steps I can see to reach that dream. Some of the goals represent baby steps. Others are a big leap that I had to take to get there. There are even some times where you are not sure which way to go. But like tanks in a battle – the worst thing to do is to stop moving. Through persistence and a belief that I can overcome whatever challenges stand between me and my dream – I just keep going. Dreams are too important to take lightly. They are worth all the energy and focus we can give them.

Even as I achieve some of my goals along the way – I am continually reevaluating my experiences and my challenges to learn and grow from them. I must take responsibility for my success and my development. It is great when family, friends, teachers and others are there to help with my dream but don't wait for that "some day" on the calendar to begin. "Some day" does not exist on any calendar. It will never be a perfect time to get going on my dream. I'll do the best I can with the resources I have and try to do even better in the future. I'm worth the investment so whatever helps me grow is a good thing – even when it is not an easy thing. If it was easy – everyone would do it!

Mistakes Were Made

I have certainly learned a great deal from some of my mistakes. LOL! The ability to make mistakes and keep going is so important to succeeding in business or any area of life. When you do make a mistake, it is tempting to give up or to get down on yourself. Be glad that you can learn from your experiences! Everyone who ever succeeded has made a pile of mistakes. The difference between them and those who are failures is that they learned from their errors and had the courage to go on. Expect to make mistakes but insist on going on – hopefully a bit smarter and a whole lot wiser for the experience.

Part of what I learned from my dream is that I had a gift. You have a special gift too! Everyone has something we can do in our own special way that can change our world.

All people who have reached for their dreams eventually figure this out. Just as the dream comes from somewhere else – we have been given a gift to make us able to do something special. That gift motivates you as you see yourself succeeding in a challenging situation. It also motivates other people who benefit from your creativity, you abilities or your enthusiasm.

I discovered that my gift included an ability to motivate and challenge other people to realize their full potential as people.

What do you want? What do you want to do? What do you want to be? What do you want to have? What do you want to contribute with your life?

Everyone who has found and is using their gift is doing something very special. While they certainly benefit as they reach their dream – using their gift creates a bit of enchantment to make the world just a bit more special that it was without that gift being used.

We live in a time that is too focused on what you can see or touch. But so much of what makes life special is the magical stuff that happens between people. We need to return to some of the enchantment or magic that each of us has. An interesting seminar series on Fairy Tales For Life (www.strategic-seminars.com) reminds us that like most areas of life – some of the most amazing things we know we learned in our earliest years. We have all sorts of magic waiting for us if we travel back in memory to some of those formative years. Growing up often clouds our vision about some of the most basic – and most important - parts of life and our dreams too.

Ignoring your dream and the gift you've received to help you get there is to make not only yourself but the world a lesser place. But as I've said before – you need to be willing to act to make it come true. Doing the same old thing that never worked over and over and expecting a different outcome – well as they say – that's one of the definitions of insanity!

So if you haven't reached your dream yet – get moving! Get started today with that basic decision. Surround yourself with people who will believe along with you in your potential. Then start taking those steps in the direction of your success. Don't wait for "someday" – it is nowhere on a calendar and like tomorrow – it will never come. Make your choice to make it happen today.

It's up to you to make your dreams come true!

Little Voices

Part of being free to enjoy who you are is to pay attention to the inner desires that speak through the little voices we all hear.

I have learned to listen to those little voices and to pay attention to my inner desires.

Have you ever had the feeling that throughout your day, your week or your month that you just have to do something because you need to do it? It's not something like showing up for work on time or paying the mortgage. It's just something that comes from deep inside you. It is part of that inner diva creating some balance between what others can tell you that you need to do and then something that you feel like you need to do.

One of my favorite times with my son is for us to lie down on the bed after supper in the fading light and watch some TV with our feet crossed and the sun shining on our faces. I knew that moment that it was the very best place in the world for me to be.

Another little inner desire is to turn up the music in the morning and sing one of my favorite songs at the top of my lungs. That gets me in the mood for the day ahead. I have a great feeling about the wonderful day to come.

Being connected to my dreams allows me to be more tuned in to who I really am, not only as a woman but as a mother, as a daughter, as a sister, as a friend. The result is that these little inner voices are free to sing into your life because you feel good about who you are.

When you start to feel comfortable with who you are – all kinds of positive things start to happen in your life. There are many reasons why this is true. Part of this is because you become a more positive person. A positive person is always more attractive and engaging in business, friendship and the rest of life.

This gives you greater potential in every area of your life. Of course it does not mean that there will not be down times or disappointments but those challenges will not become your whole story. They'll become the unusual event rather that what is normal for you.

People who have a negative mindset expect bad things to happen. No surprises there. No real disappointments – they knew it would not work out! These people understand how to play it safe by never really playing at all. The clock of their lives just keeps on ticking the same old tick-tock until it stops.

Like the traveller who flies in a jet – they get to their destinations quickly but they never really notice what passed between their departure and arrival. In contrast, the person taking a train has the luxury to slow down and notice the land, the communities and the houses as they pass by. There is something about having that grounded perspective.

It reminds me of Eeyore on Winnie The Pooh. He always had a raincloud nearby full of negative experiences. It kept him with a decidedly cloudy personality where the best he could hope for was someone could feel sorry for him. His motivation was self-pity. His best part of his day was being surprised that someone saw him. "Thanks for noticing me…" Not an inspiring character – but one we all meet everyday in business or in our communities.

Contrast the sad donkey with the bouncing Tigger. Tigger understood who he was and ran – or should I say bounced – with it! Tigger knew that the wonderful thing about Tiggers are that tiggers are wonderful things - and he could tell you so. He knew that his gift was to be that bouncy character and he celebrated it!

What are the wonderful things about being you? Maybe you can identify your best you right away.

It is a great gift to yourself and all around you if you can feel free to be your best self. Allow the spontaneous and creative whims to make your life have some sparkle. So often it is not the grand moments with great pomp and circumstance (they're fun too of course) but it is the little quiet moments walking in the woods, sitting by the lake, reading a book by the fire, eating a delicious piece of chocolate or having coffee with a friend that makes life extra special.

So often in our busy lives where every minute is scheduled (or we feel guilty that they aren't!) doing something different can make a world of difference for you.

What are the little voices you've been hearing about something you'd like to do? What inner feelings keep bubbling up to the surface? Do you act on them? Do you pretend they do not exist? Do you tell them to go away?

I really felt that. I wanted to be able to appeal to some of them and others I knew I just wasn't interested in fulfilling in that moment. You decide. Inner desires are something that you certainly will sense during the day and all of a sudden you just feel so good about being able to accomplish something just for you.

We are complex people living in a complex world of demands and often demanding people. Be sure to let the small voice with those inner desires know that if they whisper some idea that is going to refresh or invigorate you – you are ready to listen and do it! Your life and the life of those around you will be better if you do!

Power Up!

I have personal power.

The "I" in this sentence is where we must begin. I can decide to claim and use that power. Or I can decide to surrender that power to someone else. If I am powerless, I have either been fooled into believing that I had no power or I have chosen to give up my power.

Next we come to the word have. I HAVE personal power. It is already mine to use. I have it. It is part of what it means to be human. All human beings have this gift of personal power. One of the worst parts of slavery and the treatment of women in times past was that it made people feel powerless. If you feel powerless - it does not take long to feel helpless. Then it is not a long distance to believing that you are worthless.

I have PERSONAL power. That's me - a person - who has this power. It is part of my being. It may be shared or used together with others but it is my personal power. It is not mine because I have or do not have money. I may not have any high position in government or business. I may or may not belong to any powerful group. This is personal power. One person can change the world.

I have personal POWER.

Our word for power comes from the Greek word that also gives us the word dynamite. We can think of many kinds of power. There is authority based on a position of power like a government. Power also could refer to the ability to influence or sway others in the decisions and choices that they might make. There is also the idea of strength with the ability to do things. If we go back to the idea of dynamite - it certainly is a way to make changes too!

What I found about having this personal power is that I really had to recognize that I have authority and influence over my life. People may try to control me by making me feel badly about myself. I had to learn that no one has the power to tell me how to think or feel about myself unless I give them the power to do so.

We have all met people who use this in reverse. To get their way – they will try to make you feel badly about how they are feeling about what you have said or done. If they can make you feel bad about what you said or did – they can change your behavior and control you. This is not about doing something wrong or hurtful to them. Instead, this is about someone pretending to be hurt to get an advantage.

If you've ever watched professional soccer games – you've seen how people can pretend to have all sorts of wrongs done to them if they can manipulate the referee into calling a penalty on the other player. Obviously, being our best selves will usually mean that we are making a positive difference in the lives around us. Personal power is not a selfish power.

So many of our feelings get confused with our choices and what often happens is that our power disappears into someone else's world because they have manipulated and fooled us into giving it to them. You do have a choice. You do not have to give your power away.

What I know is that I have the power in one second to change what I think, what I believe, what I feel, what I do, what I have, because it's all about making a different choice. What choice is available for me in that moment? I have the power to follow and pursue something that I truly love. I have the power to have a great day and what else can we do to bring more of this into our lives.

How can we surround ourselves with this personal power?

The secret here is inside of every person. Every person's expression of their personal power will be as unique and different for them as for anyone else.

What I'm really referring to is the power for a seed to become a massive, glorious tree. I'm referring to how a little cup of water can give somebody that extra power to be able to finish a marathon run. I'm referring to the personal power that you will have when you decide that you are important and be as important as anyone else.

I have found that the secret to a joyful life is to do more of what you love every day, using your personal power. People are attracted to people who understand and use their personal power. You will be seen as someone who is transforming into a positive, whole and responsible person who knows that they can make a difference in their world.

There will be some people who will want you to be your old self. They may have liked being able to manipulate or channel your power for their purposes. They might not like seeing you get your life together. They will not be pleased to see you being able to stand on your own with confidence no matter what is happening.

When you get to this point – the people around you who count are not going to want you to change. They will be glad to see you be comfortable and at peace with who you are. They will be pleased to be with you because you will bring energy and confidence to everything you do. These are the people you need to choose to be with – just as you choose to use your personal power to make a difference.

Remember, you have the ultimate power to be and have and do.

Unleash that inner diva!

Celebrate Being A Woman

This begins by having a positive attitude about who we are as women. Women have strengths that amaze men. It is time to recognize and celebrate who we are and the difference that we make in the working world, in the arts, in government, in our communities, in our families, in our friendships.

In a world that often still discounts that value of being women – we need a fresh look. Just as in the great movie "Fried Green Tomatoes" you need to be able to shout "Towanda!"

If you are a woman – you have reason to celebrate and to be celebrated! Here are just some of the many reasons to celebrate being a woman.

1. Women carry burdens but they hold happiness, love and joy.
2. Women smile when they want to scream.
3. Women sing when they want to cry.
4. Women cry when they are happy.
5. Women laugh when they are nervous.
6. Women fight for what they believe.
7. Women stand up against injustice.
8. Women see business opportunities many men miss.
9. Women don't take "no" for an answer.
10. Women always look for a better solution.
11. Women go without so their family can have.
12. Women go to the doctor with a frightened friend.
13. Women love unconditionally.
14. Women understand that taking care of the details makes a business better.
15. Women cry when their children excel.
16. Women cheer when their friend receives an award.

17. Women are happy when they hear about a birth.
18. Women are happy when they learn about an engagement or wedding.
19. Women have hearts that break when their friend dies.
20. Women have sorrow at the loss of a family member.
21. Women find strength when they think that there is no strength left. Women understand the people who do most of the purchasing in the economy – women!
22. Women know that a hug and kiss can heal a broken heart.
23. Women come in all sizes, in all colors and shapes.
24. Women will drive anywhere for a friend in need.
25. Women can turn a cup of coffee with a hurting friend into a healing brew.
26. Women will e-mail you to show how much they care about you.
27. The heart of a woman is what makes the world spin!
28. Women bring joy.
29. Women bring hope.
30. Women show compassion.
31. Women are the keepers of the world's ideals.
32. Women are a moral support to their family and friends.
33. Women have a lot to say and a lot to give.

So as women, let us celebrate, support and care for each other. We are truly gifted and blessed.

Detox Your Relationships

Every one of us has a toxic, irrational and destructive side to our personality. This dark side can sabotage your relationships and create pain for you and others. Take charge of this aspect of your life by recognizing the signs of some of these toxic traits and choose not to think and feel this way. Yes we can make choices not only about our thinking but our emotions too.

For too long we've been told that we can't help how we feel. We can acknowledge how we're feeling at any moment – for good or bad. That keeps us from unhealthy denial. But once we've named our emotion or feeling – we then can choose to let it go or choose to move on in a different direction. We do have a choice and are not victims of our emotions.

Do you recognize any of the toxic tendencies in the examples below?

What's The Score?

The need to compete in your relationships becomes an unhealthy and ugly battle of one-upmanship. Never play the zero-sum game where if I am going to win – you must lose. How can you possibly be a winner if it is at the expense of making the person you supposedly love a loser? Solid relationships are built on sacrifice and caring, not power and control. Competitiveness can drain the joy, confidence and productivity out of any relationship.

It's Your Fault!

There is nothing wrong with constructive criticism if it is designed to improve the relationship. But it can often give way to a pattern of constant fault finding where you obsess over the flaws and imperfections rather than find value in your partner, family member or friend. Get off the other person's back and you may see them moving toward you emotionally.

Let's Compromise – You Do It MY WAY!

If you think you are always right then you're ready to fight till the end. No truer words were ever spoken than you will fight to the end - the end of your relationship. You can't be self-righteous or obsessed with control and do what's best for the relationship at the same time. We need humility in our relationships. We can always learn from others – even when we're right!

I'm Not Angry – REALLY!!!!!

When you get in an argument, do you have a killer stare, a harsh tone and hurtful words? Attack dog types may experience short-term gain getting what they want but sooner or later the target of the abuse becomes filled with bitterness and resentment. They'll learn to stay away from the barking dog. While it's easy to fall into viciousness, it's much harder to repair the damage the hurtful words and actions create.

You Are A Covert Operator

Instead of fault-finding or engaging in obvious character assassination, these toxic partners try to frustrate their partner by constantly acting like spies and undercover operators who deny they are doing anything. They are indirect and subversive in what they are doing to escape accountability and have plausible deniability if they are confronted. This takes a great deal of energy that could be used positively. Such a passive-aggressive person is just as much of an overbearing controller as the most aggressive, in-your-face person you could imagine. But they can be even more dangerous since it is hidden and denied. Beware!

Playing The Shell Game

If you lack the courage to get real about what is driving the pain and problems in your relationship, you will project your negative energy on others. This will lead you to criticize your partner about one thing when you're in fact you are really upset about something else. What is real never gets voiced, and what is voiced is never real. Sooner or later, the real issues will eventually burst forth in a nuclear blast.

I NEED You!

Needing each other is different than becoming a needy person. People who become co-dependent and who start relying on others for their identity and focus will kill any relationship. We must be whole people before we can really contribute to a relationship in a healthy way.

Taking It Too Easy

A comfort zone is a great place to visit – but you do not want to get stuck there. We need challenges to make life meaningful. Some challenges will find us without us looking. Others are there to grab. If we hide from our challenges – the comfort zone will become a death trap. Get busy growing or get busy dying!

The White Flag

Many people have entered some level of despair or depression. They have accumulated negative experiences and a negative view of life. (Of course some depression is brought on by medical, hormonal and other issues – these should be addressed through counselling and your doctor as appropriate.) But for many people, they just are down and ask what is the point of trying. When so many bad spirits crowd your life, you cannot imagine there is any way out. You become so forlorn, lonely, isolated, negative, and cynical you believe you are trapped. Reach down into the core of who you are and reach out to those who love you to turn your story around. Do not give up!

Self Respect – Even My body

What do you feel about your current body right now? When you look at yourself in the mirror - what do you see? Do you see your beautiful curves? Do you see a healthy happy amazing woman or do you see something that really is upsetting? We live in a time that celebrates a Barbie™ look even though we know Barbie™ is not real. We too often buy into a culture that strives for a perfection that can never be reached – and that is far from natural. This is a curse on young women who are trying to figure out what it means to be a woman. It is equally a curse on the middle-aged and older women who instead of aging gracefully are pulled so tight that you think they'll snap. And if they did snap – they would never feel it because of all the Botox® in their face.

When I took an honest look at myself in the mirror, I realize that for all the things that I thought I didn't love, I found many things that I did. Everything that you do is going to affect your body as a whole. And what I'm referring to by that is are you putting in healthy nourishing foods into your body or are you living this lifestyle of fatty foods that in turn don't make you feel good about you? Do you get up every day feeling good about your body? Are you wearing clothes and doing things that flatter your current figure? It really is true that beauty comes from the inside out!

Are you choosing the take-out, eat-out, fast food lifestyle? If so you are choosing to damage your body. Take time to make food. It is a way of investing in your future.

Work on a healthy body and a healthy soul. That will give you an inner beauty that will come through any body type or shape we happen to have by birth or life experiences. Celebrate who you are body, soul and spirit!

An Abundant Life

What things are available in your life that makes your life abundant? The answer to that is different for each person. But have you found out what your abundant life includes?

Let me share some what makes my life abundant. What makes me feel like I have an abundant life is being able to spend amazing quality time with my son. This means that my favorite toy and tool – my Blackberry® is off.

I have found that I had a few moments where I was spending time with my son without "spending time with my son". I felt there was always a sense of distraction even when I was not receiving a message. I felt that I wasn't really giving him the attention that he needed from me and I was missing out on some really great moments with him that would soon be gone.

Another thing that is important to me is spending time with my dog. Dogs are always ready to give you their full attention no matter what time of day or night it is. My dog is an amazing friend that makes me feel good all the time just by being around her.

My family is very, very important for me. I realize that everything that I do and everything that I am and everything that I want to contribute really is in an effort to secure their lives, as well as my own. I want my life to be a little easier so that when my son grows up and becomes a man that his life is also a little bit easier. It is what our parents hoped for us and sacrificed to make the next generation's life a bit better than there own. I really want that abundance not just of money but being loved unconditionally to flow through him.

Another thing that makes my life abundant is my work. I don't really consider it a job because I love what I do and helping people is something that has always really motivated me to do more and be more as a person. Many people associate abundance with financial abundance. Financial abundance is a positive responsibility if we have it. But it can only ever be part of the story. Financial freedom is a positive goal since it gives us more flexibility to reach some of our other dreams. But dreaming to be rich probably will keep you from the dreams that might make you wealthy but content as well.

My life is very abundant and is actually being able to contribute to the lives and well being of others.

Many years ago I used to feel that it was money that created abundance but what I realized was that many of the people that I talked with who had money were lonely because they didn't create this life of abundance first. There was no foundation to enjoy the money once they earned it.

For me, this abundance is being able to wake up in the morning with the sun on my face and get out everyday and do what I love. I love that I am able to help my son with the best education possible and help him grow to become the great man that I know he will be. That's what makes my life abundant.

So Much To Give

To be a woman is to have the opportunity to affect so many lives. We become mothers, wives, friends, and sisters. Giving is one of the most important callings that anyone can have.

If you really measured what happens in your day – you would see that you are in a constant state of giving – or responding to others who are taking. That becomes part of our choice. Better to decide where you can give than how to deal with others who are in the business of taking.

To give isn't just about money. You can give in so many other ways, your time, your advice, your thoughts. Most of all, it's really just giving of yourself as a person.

I recall a time in my life when I was giving too much. I gave so much of my time, money, energy, body, soul and spirit that I forgot about me. I burned out.

Just as we should "pay ourselves first" by setting aside money for our savings, investments and retirement before we deal with spending money – we also need to pay ourselves first emotionally, physically and spiritually too.

If you don't take care of yourself and ensure that you take time for you – you will soon have nothing to give others. Just as a corn field needs to be rotated or fallowed – we need to have time to renew ourselves. If we do not make this a priority – then like the corn field always planted with corn – you'll need a great deal of chemicals to make up for the drain on the nutrients in the soil. If we do not take time out – we will end up needing "chemicals" or other stimulants to get through. That's why so many people turn to drugs (prescription or otherwise) and alcohol to get through. They are drained.

You are an important person. Give your best, be your best - but remember that you also have to give to yourself to be able to do this.

Give your time for you to be renewed.

If this has not been your practice - start out with one minute per day that was just "you" time. You are in effect the President of your own life. Make the executive decision to protect yourself as a person. It is in your power to do this.

Everyone has different ways to renew their souls. Some do art or music. Others read a book. Some enjoy the solitude of a garden or a walk by the water. Everyone finds places that are especially good for them.

For me, it's having a nice soak in my bathtub with my favorite bath bomb and relaxing with a small TV while I watch a show that makes me laugh. I love "Will & Grace." I sip on a nice glass of ice cold water and I just relax. Add some bubbles. It is great. My hair is pinned up and just for those few minutes that I'm laying there - I can decompress and feel good about me.

As an inspirational speaker I've had many students and many colleagues come up to me and just say wow - you really gave it your all today! I am always "on" with high energy and high commitment in those moments. That is really important to me and proves the value in the contribution that I made with those people.

What a privilege!

Live Rich

How can one define living rich? Is it our bank balance or something more?

It was about four years ago that I was enjoying a Chinese dinner with one of my family members. At the end of the meal, the server brought us over our check with a couple of the traditional fortune cookies.

I reached over and opened it up. To this day, I still have the fortune message in my wallet. What it said was "It's better to live rich than to die rich." I realized it's all about my journey no matter how much money I happen to have at that moment.

In fact, our journey is to live our lives to the fullest no matter what. We tend to sweat the small stuff. The stress we feel is often about so many things that we can not change or that ultimately take care of themselves anyway.

The story is told about a man who climbed to the top of Mt. Everest. When asked why he went there - just so he could die... the climber responded that he climbed up the mountain just so he could live.

Living rich doesn't entirely mean living rich financially. Living rich is living life to the fullest everyday because we have to wonder what if there was no tomorrow? What if there wasn't an opportunity tomorrow? What if there was just today? What would you do differently? Who would you laugh with? Who would you spend time with? Who would you apologize to? What would you do in order to say that you lived your life every single day without resentment, without regrets?

Rich is being with family, fun, it's laughter, it's enjoying the people in your life. What can you do to take the time it will take to do that? Choose to live rich.

As my friend Marcia Wieder always says, "Clear out the clutter and do more of what you love!"

Give It Away

It can be a smile, a flower, a moment of your time. What will you do today to give something away without expecting anything in return?

Several years ago I was in Florida and I was walking into a store. At the time I was with a friend of mine. I went in to a store and I was trying on some clothes in the change room. As I came out to show my friend what I was wearing, a nice young lady came out of the change room wearing a lovely kind of white and red floral pattern dress. I turned with a smile on my face and I commented on how pretty I thought the dress was on her.

Throughout my conversations, we both got changed back into our original clothes and the same girl was looking at shoes that happened to be in the same pattern as the dress.

At that point, she introduced me to a friend of her family and her grandmother while telling me that she was getting married. The dress she was wearing actually was for her engagement party. Over on a shelf there was a purse that matched this dress perfectly and I made a comment about the match. The girl said "Wow! I really love that purse but we can't afford it."

So, I went over to the register and I paid for the things that I purchased and as I looked behind me and saw this girl with such a wonderful wedding day coming soon. I took off the purse off the shelf, handed it to the sales clerk and I said I want to get this purse for this girl.

I told the sales person not to give it to her until they were ready to check out and that it's a gift from the girl from Canada.

They found me in a nearby store.

What happened in that moment was a moment that I will never forget.

All three of these women started to cry as they were explaining to me that this girl's mother had passed and was not able to attend her wedding. They just looked at me and were happy and totally overwhelmed with emotion that for them – this was one of the nicest things that anybody had ever done.

What I realized in that moment was that I too was also getting emotional and I recognized that the one little thing that I gave to this girl, I will never forget either.

Like so much when we give to others - I really believe it did far more for me than it did for her on that day.

As a little tip here, I've always made it a point – way back since I was a teen – to bring something whenever I'm visiting another's home. It could be a small plant, a housewarming type of gift or even something like a poem or book. It is a small way to tell that person they are appreciated and special!

You will benefit when you give part of yourself away to others too.

Enjoy Your Successes

Success is a great place to be and certainly a great feeling to have. So what is your definition of success?

Recently I was waiting at the airport to fly to Las Vegas. I had this moment sitting there watching all the planes come in and out. So, I started to think about what makes someone successful.

In order for me to feel like I was successful I wanted to be able to go to one of my favorite places, Las Vegas. I wanted to have a limo pick me up and have some spending money. I wanted to meet some great people. I wanted to laugh, be with my friends and spend time with my son. I really wanted to have this great time where I could overlook the city and feel like somebody. I wanted to enjoy my success.

Well what was very profound in this moment for me was that everything that I had described, I was already living. It was something that in every area of my life, I realized I had already lived this way. I had already had the opportunity to entertain people. I already had the privilege to train people on being and doing and transforming their lives into something wonderful. I have amazing support in my life. I have a great business that I love. I had this great book that's being written. I have all of these things going on and all of a sudden, I felt this overwhelm of emotion and I paused wondering, wow, success to me is having love, having attention, feeling like I contribute to the lives of others.

Sometimes success is a negative for many people. We sometimes are suspicious of success or even despise it – especially in others.

So what does that mean for us to be successful? That is different for each of us – and can change as we go through the many stages on our life's journey.

Have you decided what success looks like to you at this stage in your life?

Today Is My Choice

What is a choice?

We can't live with them. We can't live without them!

For those who feel they are trapped in a situation – they will tell you they have no choice. It is a terrible feeling. Yet even in a situation where we don't feel like there is a choice – we often do have options we may not have yet noticed or considered.

On the other hand – when you have choices to make – sometimes you wish that there were not any choices. You wish that someone would make them for you so you could be sure you would make the right choice.

How do you make your choices? If you are waiting for all the possible information to guarantee that you will make the right decision – you will never get there. Choices always include some level of uncertainty – or possibility – or there would not be a real choice to make. Even when we put off making a decision, that is making a choice too. The choices you make will shape your life.

When it comes to making choices on a day to day basis, it's important to know that you have choices. Every day when you wake up in the morning, what choice are you choosing to make? Are you making a choice to have a great wonderful outstanding day or are you making a choice to have a miserable day? Our values and things we believe in, things that we know, things that we feel, things that we contribute, are all part of the choice that we make every single day.

What you will find throughout your days, weeks, months and years is that your choices are going to change depending on where you are in your life at that time. If, however, you are making choices that you know are not good for you and those in your life – then you need to change the choice.

There are some choices that we know are positive and meant to support us. We usually already know whether what we are facing is a good or bad thing. We have the power to choose – so choose well!

Live Your Values

I believe people express their values in part, based on what they buy. If I were to evaluate a credit card statement, what would it tell me about you?

Would it tell me that you live your life in restaurants? Take out, eat out? Would it tell me that you value casinos, gambling, drinking?

Or would it represent a family focus like the kid's clothes and activities and adventurous times like mini-golfing on a Saturday. Our values are what shapes and defines us no matter what our experiences at the moment. Our values are what makes us who we are and in turn allows us to be evaluated based on what we buy. What do you value? How do your values shape who you are as a woman?

Something that I thought many years ago that I valued was money. What I found about that was when I valued money everything I did was measured by money. I wasn't being me. I was being somebody else. What I realized was that the things I valued at that time turned me into somebody that I was not. I was not happy.

I'm not interested in being seen as valuable because of the money I have – rather money is just one of many tools I can use to make life better for myself and those in my world.

Dress Like You Mean It

Have you ever stopped - even for a second - to think about how what you wear communicates about who you are? What impression do you make on people when they meet you?

How do you dress? Does it reflect who you are? Does it let others around you know how vibrant, fun, kind, considerate, smart, confident you are? If you don't believe me turn the TV on some time and watch some of those reality shows about the clothes you wear, the makeup you put on the way you style your hair. It really is unbelievable.

We know that clothes really do not make the person but like the frame on a picture – what you choose to wear can either attract the person to who you really are or distract from it. Dressing well will bring the focus on you and your face rather than distracting from your beauty inside and out. Often people wear bizarre clothes as a strategy to get people to look at the accessories rather than themselves. It is often a sign of a poor self image.

You can give yourself the edge that will get you the attention you deserve.

My grandmother used to tell me all the time about how her "good" jewelry was in the safe deposit box. Are you kidding me? Why - so she could wear it twice a year? I learned this a long, long time ago. I don't believe you have to save your expensive perfume, your best jewelry and your great fancies.

I love my jewelry and my bling! I love my stuff – having it, using it, wearing it. I love my high heel shoes, and in fact wear them as often as I can. You do not need a special occasion to enjoy your belongings. I don't wait for another time or a special occasion. Remember, "someday" is not on the calendar!

Here are a few helpful hints to get you on your way:

Underneath It All

Get fitted for proper size undergarments. Yes it is going to cost a bit of money especially if you're heavier in the bust line. A good, quality bra can and will cost between $75.00 and $200.00. Don't be alarmed by this cost, believe me it is worth it to have the girls up high, in a bra that fits well. Not just in the back, but at the sides, and straps that won't cut your shoulders and arms off. My favorites are: PrimaDonna, Goddess and Lise Charmel. I love seeing my friend, June, at Bravo Fine Lingerie who makes me look and feel great underneath it all.

The Wardrobe

Do the once over inspection of your current wardrobe. Are there pieces in there that don't fit with the rest of your wardrobe choices? Are there pieces that just don't fit? If your clothes do not fit you well, and tailor to your body type, then get rid of them. I know that this is easier said then done. Many, many women have multiple "closets" in their home or storage areas for their clothes.

At one point in time, I had 4 sets of clothes. The first set was the day to day, normal wear to work and at home clothes, that well, about 70% fit me. Then in my sons room I had the "mommy clothes" the ones I wore when pregnant (that was 6 years ago) and the ones that were cozy comfy over sized and just plain not me.

In the guest room I had the "fantasy" clothing line that I wore about 15 years ago in case that if one day I was ever a size 8 again - I just might fit into again. This wardrobe is old, not trendy and some clothes still have price tags on them. The last closet is in my TV room and those clothes are the fancy, I may wear this prom dress again closet. It's full of leather jackets, suede pants, my prom dress, items that I have not worn for over 15 years. As Stevie Nicks has said, "My fashion choices were always clear. I always knew what I was going to wear on-stage."

Try everything on. Is it flattering? Does it fit you without being too tight? Do you have pieces that go together? Are your pieces fresh, assertive, colorful, do they make you feel good? If you are unsure, have a girl's night. Play dress up for your closest friend's and get their opinions. From Stacey London on television's What Not To Wear – "Wear what will fit your body today."

Shoes

Shoes – shoes!! There are 5 sets of essential shoes that every diva must own. A good walking/running shoe, a pair of stilettos (any heel height you are comfortable with…), a flat walking shoe, a pair of flip flops and a pair of dressy flat shoes.

Of course there are many more options, but these are your essentials. Spend your money wisely on shoes that are comfortable, wear well, and go with a lot of your wardrobe. Cheap shoes will not be comfortable and will in fact cost more since they may not last.

Here is my simple rule: if you're going to wear open toe shoes, please for everyone who will see your feet, get a pedicure. Even if you need to do it yourself - keep your feet looking fabulous.

Makeup

Makeup is absolutely essential. Maybe at some point you have felt it takes to long to apply or have no idea how to wear it or it costs too much money. Maybe you have decided you have no time to put it on or perhaps the truth is you may just be too lazy to bother.

Do you have any idea how a little tiny bit of makeup changes how we look? In an instant! If you are prone to never ever wear any make-up - why not try these three simple steps: mascara, a light foundation (powder or liquid), and lip gloss.

These three steps take just a minute to apply! In fact, less is usually more – especially if you do not know what you're doing. I have always believed that you want people to notice your eyes not your makeup. I do not believe there is a "special time" to wear your makeup, wear what makes you feel wonderful and fabulous. A little goes a long way!

I personally believe three things about getting yourself connected to the right makeup for you. First, go to see a professional and have them do your face up, if you can afford it. Many companies (M.A.C is my favorite!) will give you a custom makeup lesson with application for a $40.00 product purchase commitment. I started to purchase pieces, one at a time till I built the collection if have now.

Secondly, choose colours based on your eye colour, face tone, and what makes you feel good. Choose eye shadow that matches your eyes – not your clothes.

Finally, buy your makeup within your budget. If you can't afford to go to a professional counter, then have someone who is into makeup help you get started. There are many good brands that are inexpensive. Just remember that quality doesn't cost - it pays!

Feel Good

Of course, dressing in fine clothes and living the diva-chic lifestyle may be a great thing and feeling. Your public image is not just about those material things and what your wearing, it is also about who you spend time with, how to spend your money, the way you treat people, and of course how you behave while being the ultimate diva.

Let your makeup and your dress enhance your personal statement as a diva.

Diva At Work

People will often ask….how do I get my start? Do I need to go to college? Do I have to start at the bottom? I can assure you I don't have all the answers.

What I can do with confidence is share with you what worked for me. I had no idea how to run, start or get motivated to begin my company. But I did it. This is what I had going for me:

I had a vision of what I wanted.

I had a skill of communicating well, either one on one or in a group.

I had street smarts.

I do not have a college or university degree, I graduated high school and left with average grades. My dream was one day to be part of something great.

There is always a way to get into any industry or business you love or want to try. You just need to develop something a little more creative than those who may have more experience than you. Divas who are sensitive to the needs of others have a built-in advantage. Most businesses that are hugely successful begin with meeting a felt need. Someone who can recognize and design ways to help those with a need will always be successful.

You can not fear the competition. There will always be others out there who are more talented, are perceived as more beautiful or more connected than you are.

There are four fundamental principals that will assist you in getting, maintaining, and growing in your job.

Resume

First, always maintain a current resume.

Flexible Wardrobe
Secondly, keep a suit/wardrobe or something that you can interview in that is appropriate.

Take It Up A Notch
Thirdly, dress for the job you want, not the job you have.

Make An Impression
Finally, do whatever you have to do to get others to notice how capable, outgoing, smart, and creative you are. It may be surprising but if you don't tell people about how great you are they won't notice or know what you can accomplish for and with them.

As president and CEO of Representing all Women Inc., the brand that I have created follows my ideas, suggestions, opportunities, will and ultimate devotion to the countless women who I have inspired, touched, talked with and assisted on their path toward their dreams. You see this is my image that is represented. My brand.

When I am hired to speak at a major event, I have absolutely no clue who to call or how my stage, sound, TV, or satellite systems get set up or how the people get to the actual event.

What I know is my message, my value and I know the value of the people who are in attendance. I know they have troubles just like me, family issues just like me, and have personal crises just like me.

I am hands-on in every aspect but also stay away from areas of the company that do not serve my position. What I do does not require a degree or a documented history of tragedy.

The people you least expect in high ranking positions within a company often don't have the "required background" that would look impressive on a resume.

What you want to contribute is something fresh, vivacious, new and fun that often will contribute more than you think. Are you someone who is great to be around? Do you have inspiration, intelligence, dedication and more?

Do you have what I call the 3 D's - determination, dedication, and desire?

Bill Gates was asked what he thought the formula for success was. He stated that you should be at the right place at the right time, have vision of what's possible and what it will take to make it happen. Then take massive and immediate action.

I'm often asked about what is my key to success? I do not do anything I can pay someone else to do. For example, I choose not to clean house for two hours but instead I pay someone else to do it so I can spend time with my family. Look for those kinds of choices you have and start making them step by step.

Follow your passions and gifts. You'll find you're already equipped to move forward. You just need to declare it and then work to fulfill those dreams. Can you do one thing each day to help you move toward your dream?

Speak Like A Diva!

Divas usually have something important to say or share. Sooner or later you will be in front of a family gathering, a community group or a business meeting. You want to be effective in not only what you have to share but how you will share it.

In some presentations, it seems like the speaker spent thirty minutes in a freezer before they came out to communicate their organization update, corporate announcement or congratulatory speech. As they stiffly chatter out their information, the audience braces itself to hear a cold presentation.

Great public speakers have a number of natural advantages that include personality, the quality of their voice, an awareness of their audience and a sense of drama in their presentations. This combined with excellent content and experiences make them the great communicators that they are.

If you are like most people, you don't aspire to be a great public speaker. You just want to get it over with. As Jerry Seinfeld pointed out, people are more afraid of public speaking than they are of death. So, what if you need to be able to do presentations to keep you climbing the corporate ranks, add value to your organization or to just get past the dread of that part of your life?

How you prepare your presentation is important. If you clog your text with many big words that are not needed to communicate your ideas or meaningful to your audience, you've just made it difficult to succeed. Similarly, don't use words that you can not naturally pronounce. Remember, you can always issue a written statement that is very eloquent and beautifully written but beautiful writing does not always translate into beautiful speech. Written presentations and oral presentations are different.

So, what to do? Here are some quick pointers to let your diva shine through!

Use words of different sizes – that will make it more naturally interesting. Say the following sentences aloud to hear the difference:

"It is my considered opinion that any decision that advances this kind of conclusion is clearly misguided."

or…

"I am sure that this decision will take us in the wrong direction."

They both communicate the same idea but the first is very formal and includes many unnecessary components that force the listener to be a biologist as they try to "dissect the specimen".

It is helpful to memorize your speech. Audiences are usually much more impressed by a speaker who speaks without notes – if he or she speaks well. Even if you are not at that level, memorizing will give you more confidence in your presentation. Sometimes you will need to choose your words carefully and will have to read your words to be legally precise in an announcement. Even in this kind of speech, memorizing your text creates a more powerful delivery.

Here are some simple ideas that you can have alongside your note as your tip sheet to more effective speech:

Fast & Slow – Vary the speed of your presentation. Speed up and slow down. You don't want to be a train that is rattling along at the same pace.

To & Fro – Engage your whole audience. Look from side to side moving your head as well as your eyes. It is a way of acknowledging that everyone in the room is important and is noticed.

Deep & Shallow – Change the depth of where you look. Concentrate on those closer to you and those further away. Try to cover your whole group rather than having your eyes fixed on a single point at the back of the room.

High & Low – Change the pitch of your voice. Leave that monotone behind and allow your voice to go up and down. Raise it on positive and exciting points. Lower your voice on more serious statements or to emphasize concern.

Stop & Go – It is OK to pause at major points. This allows the audience time to pause too. The pause is not long – maybe just a couple of seconds but it creates a break for you and the listener.

Beyond these tips, taking a course is always a good idea. There is nothing like presenting in a safe place where you can receive valuable feedback and constructive criticism. The role-playing of doing and hearing others speak is very useful. Most people can gain insights into making a few adjustments that will improve your confidence and effectiveness.

Another helpful idea is to start paying attention when others speak. Like a judge at a competition, think about not only what the person is saying but how she or he is communicating. What are the things that they do to make it easier to understand them or to be engaged in their message? What are they doing that distracts you or turns you off? It may make the next boring corporate presentation more interesting… at least you'll know why it was boring!

Finally, there is nothing like experience. Like most of our fears – they start to disappear as you face them. If you have something worth saying – speak in a way that you will truly be heard.

Next time – do not turn down that opportunity to share your diva speech!

Starting A New Job

Are you starting a job? Okay. Starting a job is something that is going to be quite scary at first. Hopefully it will be a job that you enjoy. If that can be true for you - it won't be a just a job. Remember that you are developing a career – no matter what "jobs" you hold along the way. Even if you are taking a job that is not your preferred position because of a tough job market – never forget to enhance your career. Look for ways to better yourself while on the new job. Add courses or other experiences to make you more valuable to get that new job in your career.

Here are a few tips to get you off to the best start...

Get clear information on exactly what your tasks are to avoid the miscommunication that happens in every workplace and that could sabotage you from having a great start.

Establish what the chain of command is. Who do you go to when you have questions? Who is going to be there to answer things for you? If you're in small office, it may be different than working for a larger company where there's an actual human resources department.

Try to balance the need for being effective getting the job done with working effectively with people. Some people are great at tasks but do not know how to work with others. Others are great with people but never get any of the tasks actually finished. All jobs have some combination of these. Some roles are more people oriented while others are more about getting things done. Make sure you get things done in a way that supports and helps the people involved.

Learn about customer service. You have many customers – not just the ones who are in the public buying your company's products and services. Your customers include the people in your sales department, your office group, your boss and even the maintenance group. Having a serving attitude will make you very valuable to your group.

Believe in yourself. You are more than your job. Bring your all to work – and then leave it there. Take care of the rest of your life when you're home and at play.

The Interview Wardrobe

Some women may feel that they have to show a lot in order to get ahead. That is exactly the opposite. Less is more. In general, more skin equals less power. Find other ways to be fabulous in you without exposing a lot of body in the way you dress. People in business and people in your personal life will have more respect for you by seeing "less" of you.

Here are some practical suggestions for you. There's a possibility of being creative. If a suit is appropriate - don't make it this bright, velvet, crazy and out of control. Wear something feminine with a nice little top underneath with a vibrant color. Grab something like nice cardigan with a beautiful pencil skirt.

Be creative and use some great accessories. Add a great necklace or bracelet. Choose nice hose and heel if you can handle them.

One of my favorite dress-ups for my business is dress up jean day which is a great pair of well fitted jeans, a great shoe, a nice layered top and cardigan, or a layered tank top, or something with a fun jacket with lots of bling.

Choose your makeup carefully. Go to your department store and get some tips and analysis done to choose what works for your skin type.

Be sure to have a great haircut, apply any hair color as necessary and easy, soft make-up.

The Past and Future

The past is not your future unless you live there.
 Enough said!

Men And Their Divas

When you are in a relationship, some men can find it potentially difficult to encourage a certain behavior in his spouse or partner. I know in my marriage, I actually started to unravel my diva at some point and I wasn't really myself for a long time. Much of my marriage was actually like many women have felt - being somebody that I was not. What happened in that time was I actually kind of lost who I was or did not yet understand who I was becoming. I was so busy just letting things go and not actually being true to myself – which became destructive.

Many of the people in your life are happy with the way that things are. Some people in your life do not want you to change. But the best way to encourage the diva is just to assist her with her confidence, let her know that she is making great decisions, advise her of what you think is best without over analyzing. What often happens is that women sometimes make very little things into very big issues. Many men on the other hand do exactly the opposite.

They make very big things little and sometimes we take offense to that when they are not really expressing what they are thinking at that point. Men also process their thinking and feelings differently – and we need to know the difference.

Men can go a long way to helping their diva by giving her two things. Give her the attention she needs while she is unleashing her inner diva and second give her the praise and encouragement she needs in the process. Be specific with something that pleases you, surprises you, made you laugh or anything you notice about her. Tell her about the twinkle in her eye that is coming back.

Those types of things are how men can support their diva. For you women- communicate what it is that you want! What men really want is their wife to be happy. Happy wife = happy life!!

So What If It's A Man's World!

It was December 2, 2002. I was preparing to give a technical three-day class when I had a student come up to me and ask me where the instructor of the school was?

I extended my hand and I said, "Hi, I'm Stephanie and I'll be your instructor for the next three days." He looked at me and he said, "Oh, you're a woman." He said, "I'm not trying to offend you, I was just expecting a man."

I said, "Okay." And he then said, "No offense or anything. I've just never learned anything from a woman before."

So after I started to laugh, I just said, "Well, maybe there's going to be a first time for everything!"

But what I realized was that many women still need to prove themselves in a man's world – it distracts us from being who we are.

We have many, many, many different faces and hats that we wear in our families as mother, lover, girlfriend, sister, aunt or grandmother. These are grand titles to hold.

But to survive and thrive in a man's world – we need to continue to use the same skill sets that have served us for decades.

We need to know specifically what it is next. What's the task, function or role that we are playing?

We need to have attainable, measurable milestones and goals that we can meet and review.

We need to know where and how to get feedback on how we are doing in meeting our goals.

For many years, I thought that femininity was a sign of weakness, when in fact; it is a sign of power to most men. They did have mothers and grandmothers hopefully… We have much more power than we think we do. This is primarily just from us being able to do what we do. We have way better experience multi-tasking then men do – a very valuable trait in business and life.

On my own personal journey, I just did what I did well. I continue to do it well and better than many of my male colleagues do. I came from a place where it is a highly, highly male dominated industry. When I opened up my training center, I had people warning me that I would never make it.

I was a three-day school trainer versus the norm of two-days. I offered a hands-on approach showing them actually how to use the equipment and how to handle the work. That was unheard of at that time. But I persevered. I kept going and going. I am in my ninth year right now.

In my success, I hired a coach who could help me personally and professionally. I also chose several people both from business and from friendships that could coach me on how could I get better at this and what to do differently.

I am truly grateful for all the time and support each one gave me.

Be honest in a tactful way. Remember, that if you're ever unsure, you could always ask somebody for some input. Don't ever over-promise something that you cannot deliver. Also very important is to do whatever is necessary for you to do your job well.

After you've done this for a while – you'll realize that it's not really a man's world – and that you can play and succeed there too!

So You're In High School!

What would I say to the high school girl? Do not be so concerned about what you want to be when you grow up. I know in this day and age there is pressure to "know" what you're going to be and do for the rest of your life. But look at the stats and you realize that very few people are doing what they have always done since high school or college. I'm still deciding what I want to be when I grow up!

I know that that's changed for me over the years. When I was in grade school, I wanted to be a basketball player. I wanted to be a race car driver. I wanted to be a police officer. I wanted to be a lawyer at one point. I know that it changed actually quite often for me.

What I did know is that when I looked back in life and I evaluated all of the things I wanted to be, I knew that they all had one common denominator and that was they helped, influenced or supported people. That theme was who I really was.

If you have a passion for a certain career – work toward it. But do not be surprised or feel like a failure if you don't stay with it. Try out a variety of subjects when you're in school – who knows which one might ignite for you.

I know for myself, I did not go to any post-secondary training or education.

If you're off to college or university or some career training – find something you are truly passionate about.

Understand that you can celebrate being a woman without giving up any of your dreams about a career or life in general.

It is also important to know that you don't have to have all the answers. That's one of those short statements that is so important to get.

Find quality friends that will support you and that you can support back. You know it's really not always a contest about who has more, who has less or what brand name someone is wearing. I know for myself in high school, my friends came and went, but twenty-two years later, I still have the same best friend that I always had. Jennifer was always a friend - when I had money or when I didn't have money, when I was popular and unpopular, even going into womanhood being married with a child, she was always there for me. That's priceless.

Sometimes the decisions you make are not always going to be easy. You're going to have many, many people influence your decisions. Trying to decide what it is that you want to do is not always easy. In fact, sometimes making a decision to not make a decision is actually a good choice.

I know one of my fears for anyone in high school is that you're so influenced by doing something that you are moving forward trying to do it and you're go, go, go all the time. Then there's a moment when you've climbed to the top of the mountain and realize that it's the wrong mountain because maybe your heart is steering you somewhere else.

Too often we think that we need to be and have and do all the time when in fact maybe you just need to be. When you're in high school, you really want to spend the time and enjoy being in high school. I remember my family telling me for years that they're the best years of your life and they were right – as great as life is now.

I had a lot of really great opportunities that were often left by the wayside because I was unable to have extra support and really have people that I could rely on. Decide what your happiness is for you and follow your heart. If you're truly passionate about something, then that's the mountain you should start to climb.

On My Own

What would I say to the woman that is single again? This is actually an interesting question for me because at this time in my life, I am recently single again with a six year old child. I know what it was like to go through a period of feeling down. I went through a state of depression that often is part of the separation and divorce experience. I went through a moment where I felt that I wasn't good enough.

Tony Robbins always talks about the two fears he believes that all people have. One fear is not being good enough and the second fear is that we're not loved.

Now, I know that in my time being single again, my fear was obviously that I would be alone for the rest of my life.

But it helped that I never gave up on the fact that I am a truly a giving, warm, loving, attentive person who has much to give. I really feel I have a lot to contribute to any relationship.

I also knew that I have a better sense of who I am as a person. Many marriages suffer as people put a great deal of energy into trying to be someone we are not – although at the time I did not really understand myself as I do now. We all go through many changes as we move on along the decades of life and if we are not careful – couples can drift apart because we no longer recognize the other as the one we started with all those years ago.

When I became single again, I had to sit down and evaluate what was important for me as a woman, as a mother, as a lover, as a sister, as a daughter, so that I could really at this point get connected again with who I was and in this journey, I actually realized many, many things about myself.

The better we know who we are and how to communicate that to others – the better we will be in all our relationships – especially to those primary relationships.

The support that I received from those closest to me was very important. I had to learn to be comfortable with myself again. I had to be able to love myself again so others could love me.

Give yourself time to grieve the loss, understand who you are and what you have to offer another relationship. Do not make the mistake of putting off the grieving process by dating all the time right away. Otherwise, you will postpone the healing and growing that is waiting for you.

Work on being your best you. That will give any future relationship the best opportunity to succeed and will make your everyday life better now no matter what else is happening!

Unleashing your inner diva will help!

Some Rules for Success

No one ever procrastinated herself to the top. If you're going to do it - do it with passion. Do not constantly question and beat yourself up. Many women will tend to do that. We go along this road and then what happens is sometimes, the realist kicks in once in a while, or the doubter and it brings us down. I am too old, I'm too young, I'm too fat, I'm too skinny, I don't have enough education, etc. So, what happens is that we start to change the momentum that we actually created at one point.

Surround yourself with the right people. People who bring strong values and a diversity of thought are very valuable in our lives.

Learn when to state your opinions and go against the flow. This can go against our very instinct especially as women because we are so busy liking the thought of being liked. What happens in that moment sometimes is that when you are so busy wanting to be liked that sometimes we choose to not go against the flow for fear of ruffling feathers or having some kind of controversy. But that can be dangerous if we know deep down that something is wrong.

Do not give up! Right when you are about to burst through that moment of unleashing your diva we often run out of steam. Get your second wind - do not give up. A number of women have opted out to give up at some point simply just seeking comfort in the times when things can get a little bit more difficult and have missed out on the great opportunities that were really there.

Another step is, take time to love and be loved by the important people in your life. That will keep you grounded and centered.

I would also suggest that you possibly make yourself a checklist to inject some fun into your life. That fun can help you stay motivated and stay focused along the way!

Decide what you want that is going to fulfill you and make you happy. Are you in that moment doing what makes you happy? What I realized is that for so long I was doing things that were really not making me happy. I was doing them just for the sake of doing them. Do something different. Think of things out of the box that can help you unleash who you are. Ask your friends and ask your family what they think they think you do well or have as a gift? That will help you ignite some passion back into your life.

Finally

For all of us – the diva quest is not a place where we arrive and are done. Our inner diva will continue to grow and develop along with us. Our relationship with our inner diva also will continue to grow and mature too.

You may be at the beginning of your quest. You may have been along the road for a while. Maybe you are one of the fortunate ones (and we are all fortunate that you're there!) who has released your inner diva and you're enjoying the passion and celebration of your life as a diva.

I would invite you to share your thoughts and experiences with me. Email me at steph@representingallwomen.com

Wherever you are – never give up on yourself or the quest.

I would also challenge you to reach out to the women in your life and encourage them to discover the diva within and the wonder of the life that can be for them. Mentor younger women. Take time for the women with young children who never seem to have a minute to themselves. Share yourself with those who are down and discouraged with their life. Challenge those who need to take the risk of exploring the mysteries of life. Celebrate with others who have discovered and are using the dynamic gifts they have received and now embrace. That will not only enrich their lives but like so much of the human experience – you will receive back so much more than you are able to give.

Famous Women

We can all learn from the lives and stories of other women who have gone beyond themselves and have broken out into the world. Some are people we would like to be more like – some might be people who are very different from who we are or want to be. But any of the women who rose above the noise of their lives to touch others or break new ground have something to teach us.

Some of these names you know – others you might not. Google® them on the internet or grab a book about them to discover what made them tick and how they connected to a bigger story. You will be inspired and challenged. These are in no particular order. Who would you add to this list?

Mother Teresa	Peggy Flemming	Virginia Woolf
Mary Kay Ash	Joan of Arc	Sarah Palin
J. K. Rowling	Gertrude Stein	Mary Queen of Scotts
Michelle Obama	Eleanor Roosevelt	Jane Austen
Dolly Madison	Queen Mary	Mary the mother of Jesus
Laura Secord	Madonna	Rosa Parks
Condoleezza Rice	Golda Meir	Florence Nightingale
Chris Evert	Margaret Laurence	Emily Dickinson
Harriet Tubman	Elizabeth Taylor	Catherine the Great
Margaret Thatcher	Martha Stewart	Jane Goodall
Nadia Comaneci	Queen Victoria	Estee Lauder
Benazir Bhutto	Hilary Clinton	Indira Gandhi
Laura Bush	Coco Chanel	Anne Frank
Cleopatra	Steffi Graf	Amelia Earhart
Dorothy Sayers	Chancellor Angela Merkel	Margaret Atwood
Elizabeth I	Mary Wollstonecraft	Princess Diana
Mia Hamm	Angelina Jolie	Oprah Winfrey
Geraldine Ferraro	Tzu-hsi	Ruth Bader Ginsburg
Betsy Ross	Jackie Kennedy	Flannery O'Connor
Elizabeth II	Nancy Lopez	Beverley McLachlin
Madeleine L'Engle	Princess Grace of Monaco	Mary Pickford
Marie Curie		Helen Clark

Helpful Resources

Here are some recommended places to continue your diva quest referenced in this book.

Bravo Fine Lingerie www.bravofinelingerie.com
Doug Caporrino www.resultsthruresearch.com
Diva Coaching Academy www.representingallwomen.com
Dr. Christine Northrup, M.D www.drnorthrup.com
Omega 3 Fish Oils www.seeyourselfwell.com
ORAC Premium www.oracpremium.com
Dr. Blair Lamb, MD www.drlamb.com
Dr. Larry Komer, MD & Joan Komer www.drkomer.com
MAC Cosmetics www.maccosmetics.ca
Masters Men's Clinic www.mastersmensclinic.com
York Downs Pharmacy www.yorkdownspharmacy.com
Marcia Wieder www.dreamcoach.com
Strategic Seminars www.strategic-seminars.com
Elisa Palombi www.biglifegroup.com
Representing All Women www.representingallwomen.com
Expressions Custom Publications www.expressionscustompublications.com

How Can I Help You?

I trust that this book has been helpful to you.

Perhaps there is more that I can do for you or your group.

If you are looking for a motivational coach – I can be your Dream Coach

If your group needs a seminar, workshop or retreat speaker – I will make the occasion a powerful experience for your group.

If you would like to share with me about your journey, please share your story with me.

Email me at steph@representingallwomen.com

Call my office at **(705) 726-9987**

Visit my website www.representingallwomen.com